THE AUSTRALIAN
Women's Weekly
simply salads

The oven temperatures in this book are for conventional ovens; if you have a fan-forced oven, decrease the temperature by 10-20 degrees.

Contents

Simply Salads

Salads serve us well; they have many uses at meal times, they can be quite simple and unstructured or more stylish, they can start or finish a meal with spectacular effect. Also, serving a salad is a simple easy way to encourage everyone to eat a wide variety of vegetables (and sometimes fruit), remembering we should be eating five servings of vegies and two servings of fruit each and every day for our health and wellbeing.

A small beautiful, flavoursome salad will make a popular starter for a two- or three-course meal. Increase the quantity to suit the diners' appetites, to turn it into an impressive light meal. Or, for a more casual or family meal, start by serving a simple green leafy salad with a light dressing before the main course; this works particularly well at a barbecue while the meat or seafood is being cooked – in this case make the dressing robust in flavour.

It's a good idea to serve a small palate-cleansing salad between courses, especially if one or two of the courses are on the rich or heavy side, or if the meal is to be served over a long period of time. Salad leaves that have a slightly bitter taste are ideal for this – rocket, endive, witlof, radicchio, etc. With a little planning, salads such as these can be prepared, plated and, fridge space permitting, refrigerated and ready to serve when it's appropriate. It allows the guests and hosts alike a little breathing space, time to relax and have a chat while the cook thinks about getting the next course organised.

In the past, salads were served as accompaniments, or sides, as they're more commonly known today. They were usually part of a "cold collation" placed carefully alongside cold meat on a dinner plate – food was never stacked or served in a bowl as it is today. The plated salad often featured slices of very mild cheddar cheese plus a gherkin or two, or some pickled cocktail onions – which were available in luminous yellow, red and green – some slices of canned or home-pickled beetroot, canned pineapple rings and, for the really sophisticated, canned asparagus. Iceberg lettuce was the only lettuce available at the greengrocers, and a cook was judged by how finely the lettuce was shredded, the finer the better. If white onion – finely sliced, of course – was used in the salad it was first soaked in vinegar to remove any heat. Tomatoes and cucumbers were also sliced finely.

The dressing was usually plain vinegar – thankfully, olive oil and garlic came along and were gradually accepted. And when it comes to the dressing, a leafy salad should not look heavy – dress the salad at the last moment and use only enough dressing to make every leaf glisten. Add half the dressing to start with, then toss the salad, adding more dressing as you go, but never enough to make a puddle at the bottom of the bowl.

This cookbook is full of wonderful ideas for combining different ingredients to achieve new and exciting flavours. Some of the dressings will stand alone and become useful in any repertoire of salad recipes. Salads can make good use of leftovers; use just about any meat, poultry, seafood, cheese, pulses, grains, fruit and vegies. Bolster these with some leafy greens and fresh herbs, finish with a complementary dressing and you have a meal fit for anyone.

Salad Greens

Fresh leaves can stand alone as the perfect green salad or supply the inspirational element that sets off other salad ingredients to perfection. They go in sandwich fillings, do duty as cups or wraps to hold other foods, decorate cheeseboards and serving platters, and some have another life in delicate braises or soups or as stylish barbecue items.

RED OAKLEAF LETTUCE

RED CORAL LETTUCE

BABY COS

MIGNONETTE

OAKLEAF LETTUCE
These are mildly flavoured with loose, soft, ruffled, floppy green (above) or red-flushed leaves that look lovely with other leaves in a tossed salad. It is often described as a cut-and-come-again lettuce because, if you grow your own, you can take leaves as you need them without affecting the plant. It is available all year.

CORAL LETTUCE
Is named for its smallish, tightly crinkled leaves. It comes in green (above) or red-flushed varieties, and has a mild, slightly bitter, taste. This is a soft-leafed lettuce, but it has a frizzy mouth-feel, which makes it seem less tender than other soft lettuce. Its curly leaves help trap light oil-based dressings. Coral lettuce is available all year.

COS LETTUCE
This is a robust lettuce with a crisp spine and neutral-tasting leaves that stand up well to heavy dressings and other substantial ingredients such as eggs, fish or bacon. Regular cos (above) have a lot of leaf wastage because the outside leaves are tough and coarse, but baby cos have little wastage. Both are available all year.

BUTTER LETTUCE
These soft-leaf lettuces have a loose heart and a mild taste that harbours a very faint bitterness, making them an ideal pairing with almost any type of dressing. Available in a light-green leaf (above), or with green and reddish/bronze leaves (known as mignonette). It is a good all-round salad leaf. Both types of butter lettuce are available all year.

CURLY ENDIVE

Also called frisée because of its loose tangle of frizzy leaves; it is available in both full-size and baby forms. It has a bitter taste, though only mildly so in the tender baby leaves, which are sold as part of the baby-leaf mixture called mesclun. It is available most of the year but is at its best in winter.

MESCLUN

Also known as salad mix or gourmet salad mix, mesclun is a mix of assorted young lettuce and other baby green leaves, including baby spinach leaves, mizuna and curly endive. Mesclun is available all year round from supermarkets, usually packaged, or in loose form from greengrocers.

LAMB'S TONGUE

Also called lamb's lettuce, mâche and corn salad. It has small tender, velvety leaves and a sweet, slightly nutty, flavour. The leaves should be deep green with no yellow tinge, and need to be handled with care as they are fragile. Sold in punnets, it is available from autumn into spring.

ICEBERG LETTUCE

A crisp, refreshing lettuce with a watery crunch. Best eaten when absolutely fresh, iceberg has a very simple taste, allowing it to mix well with a great variety of flavours and textures. Use in a simple crunchy salad or with hard-boiled eggs in a sandwich. Iceberg is available all year.

RADICCHIO

This sturdy chicory comes in numerous varieties, some with red and green leaves, and some with red and white leaves. The different kinds are often called after their places of origin, such as round-headed verona and elongated treviso. Its robust, bitter leaves can also be used for braising or barbecuing. It is available all year but is best in winter.

ROCKET

Is available both wild and cultivated and also as very young or baby rocket. Its flavour has been described as roast beef with a peppery tang. Wild rocket is the hottest, cultivated rocket is less peppery because it is grown more quickly and baby rocket is the mildest. Is also known as roquette, rugula, arugula and rucola. Rocket is available all year.

MIZUNA

Also called mitsuba, this leafy Japanese herb has a crisp, aromatic flavour. Its sharply jagged leaves are similar in size and shape to baby rocket leaves, and have a mild-mustard taste, which is highlighted when paired with a miso-based or japanese-flavoured dressing. Its peak season is summer but it is available most of the year.

BABY SPINACH LEAVES

These taste much like mature spinach, having a delicate, earthy flavour, but are a little less tart. Both the stems and leaves are eaten, so choose undamaged, dark green, firm leaves and crisp stems. The leaves are perishable, so eat them soon after buying. Spinach is available all year round, but is at its peak in cooler winter months.

classic salads

greek salad

¼ cup (60ml) olive oil
1 tablespoon lemon juice
1 tablespoon white wine vinegar
1 tablespoon finely chopped fresh oregano
1 clove garlic, crushed
3 medium tomatoes (450g), cut into wedges
2 lebanese cucumbers (260g), chopped coarsely
1 small red onion (100g), sliced thinly
1 small red capsicum (bell pepper) (150g),
  sliced thinly
½ cup (75g) seeded black olives
200g (6½ ounces) fetta cheese, chopped coarsely

1 Whisk oil, juice, vinegar, oregano and garlic in large bowl; add remaining ingredients, mix gently.

prep time 20 minutes **serves** 4
nutritional count per serving 25.8g total fat
(9.6g saturated fat); 1359kJ (325 cal);
10.8g carbohydrate; 11.5g protein; 3.2g fibre

Named after Caesar Cardini, the Italian-American who tossed the first Caesar in his restaurant in Tijuana, Mexico, during the 1920s, this salad must always contain – as authenticated by Cardini's daughter – freshly made garlic croûtons, crisp cos lettuce leaves, coddled eggs, lemon juice, olive oil, worcestershire sauce, black pepper and parmesan; no single ingredient is meant to dominate. The original Caesar didn't contain bacon, hard-boiled egg, chicken breast or anchovies (the worcestershire sauce gave it that anchovy flavour).

caesar salad

½ loaf ciabatta bread (220g)
1 clove garlic, crushed
⅓ cup (80ml) olive oil
2 eggs
3 baby cos lettuce (540g), leaves separated
1 cup (80g) flaked parmesan cheese

CAESAR DRESSING
1 clove garlic, crushed
1 tablespoon dijon mustard
2 tablespoons lemon juice
2 teaspoons worcestershire sauce
2 tablespoons olive oil

1 Preheat oven to 180°C/350°F.
2 To make croûtons, cut bread into 2cm (¾ inch) cubes. Combine garlic and oil in large bowl; add bread, toss to coat in mixture. Place bread, in single layer, on oven trays; toast about 15 minutes or until croûtons are browned lightly.
3 Bring water to the boil in small saucepan; using slotted spoon, carefully lower whole unshelled eggs into water. Cover pan tightly, remove from heat; using slotted spoon, remove eggs from water after 1 minute. When cool enough to handle, break eggs into large bowl, add lettuce; toss gently to combine. Add cheese and croûtons.
4 Make caesar dressing. Pour dressing over salad; toss gently to combine. Divide among serving plates; sprinkle with freshly ground black pepper.

CAESAR DRESSING Combine ingredients in screw-top jar; shake well.

prep + cook time 50 minutes serves 4
nutritional count per serving 38.4g total fat (9g saturated fat); 2195kJ (525 cal); 28g carbohydrate; 17.7g protein; 4.6g fibre

Perfect tabbouleh relies on perfect parsley: it's imperative that the parsley is well washed to remove any grit and dried thoroughly before adding to the salad. If the parsley is too wet, the tabbouleh turns a little mushy rather than being light and tasty. Serve the tabbouleh with good-quality felafel.

tabbouleh

¼ cup (40g) burghul
3 medium tomatoes (450g)
3 cups coarsely chopped fresh flat-leaf parsley
3 green onions (scallions), chopped finely
½ cup coarsely chopped fresh mint
1 clove garlic, crushed
¼ cup (60ml) lemon juice
¼ cup (60ml) olive oil

1 Place burghul in shallow medium bowl. Halve tomatoes, scoop pulp from tomato over burghul. Chop tomato flesh finely; spread over burghul. Cover; refrigerate 1 hour.
2 Combine burghul mixture in large bowl with remaining ingredients.

prep time 30 minutes (+ refrigeration) serves 4
nutritional count per serving 14.2g total fat (2g saturated fat); 790kJ (189 cal); 9.4g carbohydrate; 3.6g protein; 5.9g fibre

caprese salad with figs

4 large tomatoes (480g), sliced thinly
4 large fresh figs (320g), sliced thinly
25 cherry bocconcini cheeses (375g), drained, sliced thinly
½ small red onion (50g), chopped finely
¼ cup firmly packed fresh basil leaves
2 tablespoons olive oil
1 tablespoon balsamic vinegar

1 Overlap slices of tomato, fig and cheese on serving plate.
2 Sprinkle with onion and basil; drizzle with combined oil and vinegar.

prep time 20 minutes **serves** 4
nutritional count per serving 23.7g total fat (10.7g saturated fat); 1367kJ (327 cal); 8.8g carbohydrate; 18.5g protein; 3.4g fibre

note Buy the best flavoured tomatoes you can find to make the most of this salad.

mixed cabbage coleslaw

⅓ cup (80ml) olive oil
2 tablespoons cider vinegar
2 teaspoons dijon mustard
2 cups (160g) finely shredded green cabbage
2 cups (160g) finely shredded red cabbage
2 cups (160g) finely shredded wombok (napa cabbage)
1 medium carrot (120g), grated coarsely
4 green onions (scallions), sliced thinly

1 Whisk oil, vinegar and mustard in large bowl; mix in remaining ingredients.

prep time 20 minutes **serves** 4
nutritional count per serving 18.4g total fat (2.6g saturated fat); 836kJ (200 cal); 4.5g carbohydrate; 2.4g protein; 4.7g fibre

waldorf salad

¾ cup (225g) mayonnaise
¼ cup (60ml) lemon juice
5 stalks celery (750g), trimmed, sliced thickly
2 medium red apples (300g), sliced thinly
1 small red onion (100g), sliced thinly
1 cup (100g) roasted walnuts
1 cup loosely packed fresh flat-leaf parsley leaves

1 Combine mayonnaise and juice in large bowl; mix in remaining ingredients.

prep time 20 minutes **serves** 4
nutritional count per serving 35.7g total fat
(3.1g saturated fat); 1852kJ (443 cal);
22.4g carbohydrate; 5.8g protein; 6.3g fibre

fattoush

2 large pitta bread (160g)
⅓ cup (80ml) olive oil
2 tablespoons lemon juice
1 clove garlic, crushed
3 red radishes (105g), trimmed, sliced thinly
½ small daikon (200g), grated coarsely
2 medium tomatoes (300g), chopped coarsely
1 lebanese cucumber (130g), chopped coarsely
1 small red onion (100g), sliced thinly
1 small green capsicum (bell pepper) (150g),
  chopped coarsely
1 cup loosely packed fresh mint leaves
1 cup loosely packed fresh flat-leaf parsley leaves

1 Preheat grill (broiler) to hot.
2 Place bread on oven tray; grill until crisp. Break bread into pieces.
3 Whisk oil, juice and garlic in large bowl. Mix in half the bread and remaining ingredients.
4 Serve fattoush sprinkled with remaining bread.

prep + cook time 20 minutes **serves** 4
nutritional count per serving 19.7g total fat
(2.7g saturated fat); 1367kJ (327 cal);
28.1g carbohydrate; 6.8g protein; 5.8g fibre

panzanella

1 litre (4 cups) water
250g (8 ounces) stale sourdough bread, cut into
  2cm (¾ inch) slices
2 large tomatoes (440g), chopped coarsely
1 small red onion (100g), sliced thinly
2 lebanese cucumbers (260g), chopped coarsely
1 cup firmly packed fresh basil leaves
2 tablespoons olive oil
2 tablespoons red wine vinegar
1 clove garlic, crushed

1 Place the water in large shallow bowl; briefly
dip bread slices into water. Pat dry with absorbent
paper; tear bread into large chunks.
2 Place bread in large bowl with remaining
ingredients; toss gently.

prep time 20 minutes serves 4
nutritional count per serving 11g total fat
(1.5g saturated fat); 1104kJ (264 cal);
33.2g carbohydrate; 7.5g protein; 6g fibre

salade niçoise

200g (6½ ounces) baby green beans
2 tablespoons olive oil
1 tablespoon lemon juice
2 tablespoons white wine vinegar
4 medium tomatoes (600g), cut into wedges
4 hard-boiled eggs, quartered
425g (13½ ounces) canned tuna in springwater,
 drained, flaked
½ cup (80g) rinsed, drained caperberries
½ cup (60g) seeded small black olives
¼ cup firmly packed fresh flat-leaf parsley leaves
440g (14 ounces) canned drained whole baby new
 potatoes, rinsed, halved

1 Boil, steam or microwave beans until tender;
drain. Rinse under cold water; drain.
2 Whisk oil, juice and vinegar in large bowl; add
beans and remaining ingredients, toss gently.

prep + cook time 20 minutes **serves** 4
nutritional count per serving 16.9g total fat
(3.7g saturated fat); 1522kJ (364 cal);
19.5g carbohydrate; 30.9g protein; 5.2g fibre

warm thai beef salad

800g (1½-pound) piece beef rump steak
1 teaspoon peanut oil
250g (8 ounces) bean thread vermicelli
1 telegraph (hothouse) cucumber (400g),
  halved lengthways, sliced thinly
1 large red capsicum (bell pepper) (350g),
  sliced thinly
1 small red onion (100g), sliced thinly
1 fresh long red chilli, sliced thinly
1 cup firmly packed fresh mint leaves
1 cup firmly packed fresh coriander leaves
  (cilantro)

LIME DRESSING
1 tablespoon coarsely chopped fresh coriander
  (cilantro) root and stem mixture
5 cloves garlic, chopped coarsely
1 teaspoon black peppercorns
½ cup (125ml) lime juice
1 tablespoon fish sauce
1 tablespoon grated palm sugar
2 x 10cm (4 inch) sticks fresh lemon grass (40g),
  chopped coarsely

1 Brush beef, both sides, with oil; cook on heated grill plate (or grill or barbecue) until cooked as desired. Cover beef; stand 5 minutes.
2 Place vermicelli in large heatproof bowl, cover with boiling water; stand until tender, drain. Cut vermicelli into random lengths into same bowl.
3 Meanwhile, make dressing.
4 Slice beef thinly; combine in large bowl with half the dressing and remaining ingredients. Drizzle remaining dressing over vermicelli. Divide vermicelli among shallow serving bowls; top with salad.

LIME DRESSING Blend or process ingredients until chopped finely.

prep + cook time 30 minutes serves 6
nutritional count per serving 10.6g total fat (4.2g saturated fat); 1597kJ (382 cal); 34g carbohydrate; 35.3g protein; 3.4g fibre

To prepare the coriander root and stem mixture, wash the coriander under cold water, removing any dirt clinging to the roots; scrape the roots with a small flat knife to remove some of the outer fibrous skin. Chop the coriander roots and stems together to obtain the amount specified.
The dressing can be made several hours ahead. The salad can be prepared leaving only the steak to cook and the vermicelli to soften.

asian salads

honey chicken, tamarind and lime salad

¼ cup (60ml) peanut oil
¼ cup (60ml) tamarind concentrate
1 tablespoon honey
2 teaspoons dark soy sauce
½ teaspoon finely grated lime rind
1 tablespoon lime juice
1 clove garlic, crushed
800g (1½ pounds) chicken breast fillets
½ small wombok (napa cabbage) (350g), trimmed,
  shredded finely
4 green onions (scallions), sliced thinly
500g (1 pound) red radishes, trimmed, sliced
  thinly, cut into matchsticks
2 lebanese cucumbers (260g), halved widthways,
  seeded, cut into matchsticks
½ cup loosely packed fresh mint leaves
½ cup loosely packed fresh coriander leaves
  (cilantro)
⅔ cup (50g) fried shallots

HONEY LIME DRESSING
1 tablespoon honey
2 tablespoons lime juice
1 teaspoon sesame oil
1 tablespoon dark soy sauce
1 fresh long red chilli, chopped finely

1   Combine 1 tablespoon of the oil, tamarind, honey, sauce, rind, juice, garlic and chicken in large bowl, cover; refrigerate 3 hours or overnight.
2   Make honey lime dressing.
3   Heat remaining oil in large frying pan; cook chicken mixture, in batches, until cooked through. Cover chicken; stand 5 minutes, then slice chicken thickly. Cover to keep warm.
4   Meanwhile, combine dressing in large bowl with remaining ingredients. Divide salad among plates; top with chicken.

HONEY LIME DRESSING Combine ingredients in screw-top jar; shake well.

prep + cook time 55 minutes (+ refrigeration)
serves 4
nutritional count per serving 27g total fat
(6.1g saturated fat); 2144kJ (513 cal);
19.4g carbohydrate; 46.3g protein; 4.3g fibre

You can poach, shred and refrigerate the chicken a day ahead, and you can also prepare the dressing and salad vegetables a day ahead. Keep them refrigerated, then simply combine with the noodles when you're ready. Or, poach and shred the chicken, and use it warm with the salad ingredients and noodles.

chicken and vermicelli noodle salad

2 litres (8 cups) water
800g (1½ pounds) chicken breast fillets
200g (6½ ounces) rice vermicelli
150g (4½ ounces) snow peas
8 green onions (scallions)
2 medium carrots (240g)
½ medium wombok (napa cabbage) (500g), shredded finely
2 cups (160g) bean sprouts
1 cup firmly packed fresh mint leaves
1 cup firmly packed fresh coriander leaves (cilantro)
½ cup (70g) roasted unsalted peanuts, chopped coarsely

SWEET CHILLI DRESSING
½ cup (125ml) lime juice
2 tablespoons fish sauce
3 teaspoons sambal oelek
2 teaspoons sesame oil
1 tablespoon light brown sugar
1 clove garlic, crushed

1 Bring the water to the boil in large saucepan; add chicken. Simmer, uncovered, about 10 minutes or until chicken is cooked. Cool chicken in poaching liquid 10 minutes; drain. Using two forks, shred chicken coarsely.
2 Place vermicelli in large heatproof bowl, cover with boiling water; stand until tender, drain. Rinse under cold water, drain.
3 Meanwhile, make sweet chilli dressing.
4 Slice snow peas and onions diagonally into thin strips. Halve carrots crossways; cut into matchsticks. Combine peas, onion, carrot, wombok, sprouts, herbs and chicken in large bowl with vermicelli; drizzle with dressing. Serve salad sprinkled with nuts.

SWEET CHILLI DRESSING Combine ingredients in screw-top jar; shake well.

prep + cook time 40 minutes serves 6
nutritional count per serving 15.1g total fat (3.1g saturated fat); 1772kJ (424 cal); 30.9g carbohydrate; 37.7g protein; 6.4g fibre

vietnamese marinated beef salad

400g (12½ ounces) beef fillet, sliced thinly
2 teaspoons finely grated lime rind
¼ cup (60ml) lime juice
1 tablespoon fish sauce
1 tablespoon grated palm sugar
1 clove garlic, crushed
10cm (4 inch) stick fresh lemon grass (20g),
  crushed, chopped finely
1 fresh small red thai (serrano) chilli, chopped finely
2cm (¾ inch) piece fresh ginger (10g), grated
¼ cup (60ml) peanut oil
1 cup (80g) bean sprouts
1 medium red capsicum (bell pepper) (200g),
  sliced thinly
1 medium carrot (120g), cut into matchsticks
1 cup loosely packed fresh vietnamese mint leaves
1 cup loosely packed fresh coriander leaves
  (cilantro)

1 Combine beef, rind, juice, sauce, sugar, garlic,
lemon grass, chilli, ginger and 2 tablespoons of
the oil in medium bowl; cover, refrigerate 1 hour.
2 Heat remaining oil in wok; stir-fry beef mixture,
in batches, until browned.
3 Combine beef with remaining ingredients in
large bowl.

prep + cook time 25 minutes (+ refrigeration)
serves 4
nutritional count per serving 20g total fat
(5g saturated fat); 1325kJ (317 cal);
8.7g carbohydrate; 24.1g protein; 3.6g fibre

asian duck salad

1kg (2-pound) chinese barbecued duck
150g (4½ ounces) snow peas, sliced thinly
1 green mango (350g), sliced thinly
3 shallots (75g), sliced thinly
125g (4 ounces) mizuna
⅓ cup firmly packed fresh mint leaves
⅓ cup firmly packed fresh coriander leaves
   (cilantro)
1 fresh long red chilli, sliced thinly

THAI DRESSING
2 tablespoons fish sauce
2 tablespoons grated palm sugar
⅓ cup (80ml) lime juice
2 teaspoons peanut oil

1 Remove meat, leaving skin on, from duck;
discard bones. Chop meat coarsely; place in large
bowl with remaining ingredients.
2 Make thai dressing. Pour dressing over salad;
toss gently to combine.

THAI DRESSING Combine ingredients in screw-top
jar; shake well.

prep time 25 minutes serves 4
nutritional count per serving 35.2g total fat
(10g saturated fat); 2082kJ (498 cal);
17.8g carbohydrate; 28.1g protein; 3.3g fibre

Green (unripe) papayas are readily available in various sizes at many greengrocers, Asian food shops and markets. Select one that is very hard and slightly shiny, which indicates it's fresh but not too unripe to grate or chop.

pickled green papaya salad

1 cup (250ml) water
½ cup (125ml) rice vinegar
½ cup (110g) white sugar
1 teaspoon salt
1 fresh long red chilli, halved lengthways
1 small green papaya (650g)
150g (4½ ounces) sugar snap peas
100g (3 ounces) bean thread vermicelli
½ small pineapple (450g), quartered, sliced thinly
1 small red onion (100g), sliced thinly
1 cup firmly packed fresh mint leaves
1 fresh long red chilli, sliced thinly

PALM SUGAR DRESSING
¼ cup (60ml) lime juice
2 tablespoons grated palm sugar

1   Combine the water, vinegar, sugar, salt and halved chilli in small saucepan; bring to the boil. Reduce heat; simmer, uncovered, 5 minutes. Strain into small jug; discard solids. Cool 10 minutes.
2   Meanwhile, peel papaya. Quarter lengthways, discard seeds. Grate papaya coarsely.
3   Place papaya in medium bowl with vinegar mixture; stand, covered, 1 hour.
4   Boil, steam or microwave peas until just tender; drain. Place noodles in medium heatproof bowl, cover with boiling water; stand until just tender, drain. Rinse under cold water; drain. Using kitchen scissors, cut noodles into random lengths.
5   Make palm sugar dressing.
6   Place drained papaya, peas and noodles in medium bowl with pineapple, onion, mint and dressing; toss gently.
7   Divide salad between serving bowls; top with sliced chilli.

PALM SUGAR DRESSING   Combine ingredients in screw-top jar; shake well.

prep + cook time 30 minutes (+ standing) serves 4
nutritional count per serving 0.4g total fat
(0g saturated fat); 577kJ (138 cal);
29g carbohydrate; 3.1g protein; 6.4g fibre

warm tuna and green tea noodle salad

2 x 10cm (4 inch) sticks fresh lemon grass (40g),
  chopped finely
1 tablespoon light soy sauce
2 teaspoons grated palm sugar
2 tablespoons lime juice
3 x 155g (5 ounce) tuna steaks
200g (6½ ounces) dried green tea soba noodles
2 teaspoons sesame oil
1 cup firmly packed fresh coriander leaves
  (cilantro)

1 Blend or process lemon grass, sauce, sugar and
1 tablespoon of the juice until smooth.
2 Combine tuna and half the lemon grass mixture
in large bowl. Cook tuna on heated oiled grill plate
(or grill or barbecue). Cover tuna; stand 5 minutes
then slice thinly.

3 Meanwhile, cook noodles in large saucepan of
boiling water until tender; drain.
4 Whisk remaining lemon grass mixture, oil and
remaining juice in large bowl. Add tuna, noodles
and coriander; mix gently.

prep + cook time 25 minutes **serves** 4
nutritional count per serving 9.5g total fat
(3.1g saturated fat); 1584kJ (379 cal);
36g carbohydrate; 35.4g protein; 2.4g fibre

notes You can use light brown sugar instead of
the palm sugar.
Green tea soba noodles are flavoured with
powdered green tea and are available dried from
Asian food stores and the Asian food section of
most large supermarkets. Use plain dried soba
noodles, if you prefer.

thai-style seared tuna and green mango salad

1 green mango (350g)
2 teaspoons sesame oil
800g (1½ pounds) tuna steaks, cut into 3cm
  (1¼ inch) pieces
½ teaspoon dried chilli flakes
2 tablespoons roasted sesame seeds
2 cups (100g) snow pea sprouts
½ cup firmly packed fresh coriander leaves
  (cilantro)
½ cup firmly packed fresh mint leaves
½ small red onion (50g), sliced thinly

LIME AND GINGER DRESSING
¼ cup (60ml) lime juice
3cm (1¼ inch) piece fresh ginger (15g), grated
1 tablespoon fish sauce

1 Make lime and ginger dressing.
2 Using vegetable peeler, slice mango into
thin ribbons.
3 Combine oil and fish in medium bowl. Cook fish
on heated oiled grill plate (or grill or barbecue).
4 Return fish to same cleaned bowl with chilli and
seeds; mix gently.
5 Combine mango with remaining ingredients
and dressing in medium bowl. Serve salad topped
with fish.

LIME AND GINGER DRESSING Combine
ingredients in screw-top jar; shake well.

prep + cook time 30 minutes serves 4
nutritional count per serving 17.8g total fat
(5.4g saturated fat); 1894kJ (453 cal);
15.5g carbohydrate; 55.5g protein; 3.7g fibre

soba salad with seaweed, ginger and vegetables

20g (¾ ounce) wakame
200g (6½ ounces) dried soba noodles
2 lebanese cucumber (260g), seeded, cut into
  matchsticks
2 small carrots (140g), cut into matchsticks
1 tablespoon toasted sesame seeds
3 green onions (scallion), sliced thinly
2cm (¾ inch) piece fresh ginger (10g), grated
2 teaspoons sesame oil
¼ cup (60ml) lime juice
1 tablespoon tamari

1 Place wakame in small bowl, cover with cold
water; stand about 10 minutes or until wakame
softens, drain. Discard any hard stems; chop coarsely.
2 Meanwhile, cook noodles in small saucepan of
boiling water until just tender; drain. Rinse under
cold water; drain. Chop noodles coarsely.
3 Place wakame and noodles in medium bowl with
remaining ingredients; toss gently to combine. If
you like, sprinkle with extra sesame seeds to serve.

prep + cook time 30 minutes **serves** 4
nutritional count per serving 4.6g total fat
(0.6g saturated fat); 1003kJ (240 cal);
37.5g carbohydrate; 8.1g protein; 6.1g fibre

Wakame, a bright-green seaweed usually sold in dried form, is used
in soups, salads and seasonings. Dried wakame must be softened by
soaking for about 10 minutes, and any hard stems are then discarded.
It is available from most Asian food stores.
Soba is a Japanese noodle, similar in appearance to spaghetti, made
from buckwheat.

barbecued pork and crunchy noodle salad

10 trimmed red radishes (150g), sliced thinly,
  cut into matchsticks
1 large red capsicum (bell pepper) (350g),
  sliced thinly
2 baby buk choy (300g), sliced thinly
6 green onions (scallions), sliced thinly
1 cup (80g) bean sprouts
½ cup (70g) roasted slivered almonds
2 x 100g (3 ounce) packets fried noodles
400g (12½ ounces) chinese barbecued pork,
  sliced thinly

SWEET-SOUR DRESSING
¼ cup (60ml) peanut oil
2 tablespoons white vinegar
2 tablespoons light brown sugar
2 tablespoons light soy sauce
1 teaspoon sesame oil
1 clove garlic, crushed

1 Combine ingredients for sweet-sour dressing
in screw-top jar; shake well.
2 Combine salad ingredients in large bowl
with dressing.

prep time 20 minutes **serves** 6
nutritional count per serving 29.7g total fat
(7.6g saturated fat); 1789kJ (428 cal);
17.6g carbohydrate; 20.4g protein; 6.1g fibre

salmon and pickled ginger salad

100g (3 ounces) rice vermicelli
800g (1½ pounds) salmon fillets, skin on
3 shallots (75g), sliced thinly
1 cup loosely packed fresh coriander leaves
  (cilantro)
2 tablespoons drained pickled ginger in syrup,
  sliced finely

SESAME SOY DRESSING
1 tablespoon sesame seeds, toasted
2 tablespoons lemon juice
1 tablespoon pickled ginger syrup
1 tablespoon light soy sauce
1 tablespoon kecap manis
2 teaspoons sesame oil
2 teaspoons olive oil

1 Place vermicelli in large heatproof bowl; cover with boiling water. Stand until just tender; drain. Rinse under cold water; drain.
2 Meanwhile, cook fish, skin-side down, on heated oiled grill plate (or grill or barbecue) about 5 minutes or until skin is crisp. Turn fish; cook about 4 minutes or until cooked as desired. Lift skin from fish; cook skin on grill plate until crisp. Slice skin finely; flake fish into large pieces.
3 Make sesame soy dressing.
4 Combine vermicelli, shallot, coriander, ginger and half the dressing in large bowl; divide among serving plates. Top with fish, drizzle with remaining dressing; sprinkle with crisp salmon skin.

SESAME SOY DRESSING Combine ingredients in small bowl.

prep + cook time 35 minutes serves 4
nutritional count per serving 20.7g total fat (4g saturated fat); 1793kJ (429 cal); 17.7g carbohydrate; 42.3g protein; 1.3g fibre

For the pickled ginger syrup in the dressing, use the syrup drained from the pickled ginger in the salad.
The salmon skin gets wonderfully crunchy when cooked twice on the grill, as we do in this recipe; this provides added texture and flavour.

barbecued duck and lychee salad

1kg (2-pound) chinese barbecued duck
565g (1¼ pounds) canned lychees in syrup,
  drained, halved
6 trimmed red radishes (90g), sliced thinly
60g (2 ounces) mizuna, torn
½ cup coarsely chopped fresh mint
2 green onions (scallions), sliced thinly

KAFFIR LIME AND CHILLI DRESSING
¼ cup (60m) lime juice
1 tablespoon olive oil
1 teaspoon fish sauce
1 teaspoon grated palm sugar
2 fresh kaffir lime leaves, sliced thinly
1 fresh small red thai (serrano) chilli, chopped finely
1 clove garlic, crushed

1 Remove skin and meat from duck; discard
bones. Slice skin thickly and meat thinly.
2 Make kaffir lime and chilli dressing.
3 Combine duck, dressing and remaining
ingredients in large bowl.

KAFFIR LIME AND CHILLI DRESSING Combine
ingredients in screw-top jar; shake well.

prep time 25 minutes serves 4
nutritional count per serving 41.9g total fat
(11.8g saturated fat); 2416kJ (578 cal);
20.3g carbohydrate; 29.6g protein; 2.7g fibre

five-spiced pork and nashi in chilli plum dressing

600g (1¼ pounds) pork fillets, trimmed
2 teaspoons vegetable oil
1 teaspoon five-spice powder
300g (9½ ounces) mizuna
2 green onions (scallions), sliced thinly
2 medium nashi (400g), sliced thinly

CHILLI PLUM DRESSING
¼ cup (60ml) plum sauce
1 tablespoon water
1 tablespoon lemon juice
1 fresh long red chilli, sliced thinly

1   Combine pork, oil and spice in large bowl; refrigerate 3 hours or overnight.
2   Make chilli plum dressing.
3   Cook pork on heated oiled grill plate (or grill or barbecue) about 20 minutes. Cover pork; stand 10 minutes, then slice thickly.
4   Combine mizuna, onion and nashi in large bowl with two-thirds of the dressing. Serve salad topped with pork; drizzle with remaining dressing.

CHILLI PLUM DRESSING Combine ingredients in small bowl.

prep + cook time 30 minutes (+ refrigeration)
serves 4
nutritional count per serving 14.8g total fat (4.3g saturated fat); 1522kJ (364 cal); 22.5g carbohydrate; 33.3g protein; 3.1g fibre

Fried shallots, served as a condiment at Asian mealtimes or sprinkled over just-cooked food, provide an extra crunchy finish to stir-fries, salads or curries. Available at all Asian grocery stores; once opened, they will keep for months if stored in a tightly sealed glass jar.

vietnamese chicken salad

500g (1 pound) chicken breast fillets
1 large carrot (180g)
½ cup (125ml) rice wine vinegar
2 teaspoons salt
2 tablespoons caster (superfine) sugar
1 medium white onion (150g), sliced thinly
1½ cups (120g) bean sprouts
2 cups (160g) finely shredded savoy cabbage
¼ cup firmly packed fresh vietnamese mint leaves
½ cup firmly packed fresh coriander leaves
  (cilantro)
1 tablespoon crushed roasted peanuts
2 tablespoons fried shallots

VIETNAMESE DRESSING
2 tablespoons fish sauce
¼ cup (60ml) water
2 tablespoons caster (superfine) sugar
2 tablespoons lime juice
1 clove garlic, crushed

1 Place chicken in medium saucepan of boiling water; return to the boil. Reduce heat; simmer, uncovered, about 10 minutes or until chicken is cooked through. Cool chicken in poaching liquid 10 minutes; discard liquid. Shred chicken coarsely.
2 Meanwhile, cut carrot into matchstick-sized pieces. Combine carrot in large bowl with vinegar, salt and sugar, cover; stand 5 minutes. Add onion, cover; stand 5 minutes. Add sprouts, cover; stand 3 minutes. Drain pickled vegetables; discard liquid.
3 Place pickled vegetables in large bowl with chicken, cabbage, mint and coriander.
4 Make vietnamese dressing. Pour dressing over salad in bowl; toss gently to combine. Sprinkle with nuts and shallots.

VIETNAMESE DRESSING Place ingredients in screw-top jar; shake well.

prep + cook time 35 minutes serves 4
nutritional count per serving 8.9g total fat (2.3g saturated fat); 1271kJ (304 cal); 24.3g carbohydrate; 31g protein; 5.1g fibre

This recipe can be prepared up to step 5 the day before serving.

crisp pork belly and wombok salad

2 cups (500ml) salt-reduced chicken stock
⅓ cup (80ml) chinese cooking wine
½ cup (125ml) lime juice
¼ cup (60ml) japanese soy sauce
2 dried red chillies
2 star anise
1 tablespoon coarsely chopped fresh coriander
  (cilantro) root and stem mixture (see note page 18)
2cm (¾ inch) piece fresh ginger (10g), sliced thinly
2 cloves garlic, halved
2 fresh kaffir lime leaves, torn
800g (1½-pound) piece boneless pork belly
¼ cup (60ml) oyster sauce
⅓ cup (90g) firmly packed grated palm sugar
2 tablespoons fish sauce
1 tablespoon peanut oil
2 fresh long red chillies, chopped finely
2cm (¾ inch) piece fresh ginger (10g), grated
1 clove garlic, crushed
½ medium wombok (napa cabbage) (500g),
  shredded finely
1 medium red capsicum (bell pepper) (200g),
  sliced thinly
1 large carrot (180g), sliced thinly
1 cup (80g) bean sprouts
2 green onions (scallions), sliced thinly
½ cup loosely packed fresh coriander leaves
  (cilantro)
½ cup loosely packed fresh vietnamese mint leaves
½ cup (70g) roasted unsalted peanuts,
  chopped coarsely
¼ cup (20g) fried shallots

1 Combine stock, wine, half the juice, soy sauce, dried chillies, star anise, coriander root and stem mixture, sliced ginger, halved garlic, lime leaves and pork in large deep flameproof dish; bring to the boil. Reduce heat; simmer, covered tightly, about 1½ hours or until pork is tender.
2 Remove pork from dish. Strain broth through muslin-lined sieve into medium saucepan; discard solids. Bring broth to the boil; boil, uncovered, 10 minutes.
3 Slice pork lengthways into 1cm-thick (½ inch) slices. Combine pork with half the broth and oyster sauce in large bowl. Cover; refrigerate 2 hours.
4 Meanwhile, to make dressing, stir palm sugar into remaining broth; bring to the boil, stirring until sugar dissolves. Reduce heat; simmer, uncovered, about 5 minutes or until thickened slightly. Remove from heat; stir in remaining juice, fish sauce, oil, fresh chilli, grated ginger and crushed garlic. Cool dressing.
5 Preheat oven to 240°C/475°F. Oil two oven trays, line with baking paper.
6 Drain pork; discard marinade. Place pork, in single layer, on trays; cook, uncovered, turning occasionally, about 20 minutes or until crisp. Cut pork slices into 2cm (¾ inch) pieces.
7 Meanwhile, place wombok, capsicum, carrot, sprouts, onion, coriander leaves, mint, nuts and dressing in large bowl; add pork, toss gently.
8 Divide salad among serving bowls, sprinkle with fried shallots.

prep + cook time 3 hours (+ refrigeration) serves 4
nutritional count per serving 58.7g total fat
(17.6g saturated fat); 4009kJ (959 cal);
37.7g carbohydrate; 64.8g protein; 16.8g fibre

mediterranean salads

char-grilled mediterranean vegetables in fresh oregano dressing

1 medium red capsicum (bell pepper) (200g)
1 medium yellow capsicum (bell pepper) (200g)
1 large red onion (300g), halved, cut into wedges
1 small kumara (orange sweet potato) (250g), sliced thinly lengthways
2 baby eggplants (120g), sliced thinly lengthways
2 medium zucchini (240g), halved lengthways
340g (11 ounce) jar artichoke hearts, drained, halved
100g (3 ounces) seeded black olives
1 small radicchio (150g), leaves separated

FRESH OREGANO DRESSING
¼ cup (60ml) olive oil
2 tablespoons red wine vinegar
2 tablespoons lemon juice
2 cloves garlic, crushed
1 tablespoon finely chopped fresh oregano leaves

1 Quarter capsicums, remove and discard seeds and membranes; cut capsicum into thick strips.
2 Make fresh oregano dressing.
3 Cook capsicum, onion, kumara, eggplant, zucchini and artichoke, in batches, on heated oiled grill plate (or grill or barbecue) until browned.
4 Combine char-grilled vegetables, olives and dressing in large bowl; toss gently to combine. Serve with radicchio.

FRESH OREGANO DRESSING Combine ingredients in screw-top jar; shake well.

prep + cook time 55 minutes serves 4
nutritional count per serving 14.8g total fat (2g saturated fat); 1104kJ (264 cal); 22.8g carbohydrate; 6.4g protein; 7.6g fibre

quail with radicchio and pear salad

4 quails (640g)
16 fresh sage leaves
4 slices prosciutto (60g), halved lengthways
2 teaspoons olive oil
1 ruby red grapefruit (350g)
30g (1 ounce) butter
2 small pears (360g), cut into wedges
2 small radicchio (300g), leaves separated

BALSAMIC DRESSING
2 tablespoons balsamic vinegar
1 tablespoon olive oil
1 clove garlic, crushed

1 Using kitchen scissors, cut along sides of each quail's backbone; discard backbones. Halve each quail along breastbone. Place 2 sage leaves on each quail half; wrap with a slice of prosciutto.
2 Heat oil in large frying pan; cook quail, in batches, about 10 minutes or until cooked.
3 Meanwhile, segment grapefruit over small bowl; reserve 1 tablespoon of juice for dressing.
4 Make balsamic dressing.
5 Heat butter in medium frying pan; add pear, cook about 4 minutes or until tender.
6 Divide radicchio, grapefruit and pear among serving plates; top with quail, drizzle with dressing.

BALSAMIC DRESSING Combine vinegar, oil, garlic and reserved grapefruit juice in screw-top jar; shake well.

prep + cook time 45 minutes serves 4
nutritional count per serving 25.1g total fat (9g saturated fat); 1522kJ (364 cal); 13.6g carbohydrate; 19.4g protein; 3.9g fibre

bocconcini salad with semi-dried tomato pesto

270g (8½ ounce) jar semi-dried tomatoes in oil
¼ cup (20g) coarsely grated parmesan cheese
1 tablespoon roasted pine nuts
1 fresh long red chilli, chopped coarsely
2 tablespoons lemon juice
⅓ cup (80ml) pouring cream
630g (1¼ pounds) cherry bocconcini cheese, drained
1 cup (150g) plain (all-purpose) flour
2 eggs, beaten lightly
1 cup (100g) packaged breadcrumbs
vegetable oil, for deep-frying
4 witlof (belgian endive) (500g), leaves separated
30g (1 ounce) mizuna

1   Drain tomatoes over small bowl; reserve ½ cup of the oil. Roughly chop half the tomatoes; slice remaining tomatoes into thin strips.
2   Blend chopped tomatoes, parmesan, nuts, chilli and juice until smooth. With motor operating, gradually add reserved oil in a thin, steady stream; blend until smooth. Transfer pesto to small jug; stir in cream.
3   Coat bocconcini in flour; shake off excess. Dip in egg, then coat in breadcrumbs.
4   Heat oil in medium deep saucepan; deep-fry bocconcini, in batches, until browned lightly. Drain on absorbent paper.
5   Divide witlof among serving plates; top with bocconcini then sprinkle with tomato strips and mizuna. Drizzle over pesto to serve.

prep + cook time 45 minutes **serves** 4
nutritional count per serving 52.5g total fat
(25.1g saturated fat); 3867kJ (925 cal);
60.7g carbohydrate; 47g protein; 11.5g fibre

You need to buy three tubs of cherry bocconcini cheese for this recipe.

warm balsamic mushroom and pancetta salad

8 slices pancetta (120g)
½ cup (125ml) balsamic italian dressing
⅓ cup water
500g (1 pound) small button mushrooms
1 teaspoon fresh thyme leaves
90g (3 ounces) mesclun
90g (3 ounces) fetta cheese, crumbled

1 Cook pancetta in heated oiled large frying pan until crisp. When cool enough to handle, break into large pieces.
2 Heat dressing and the water in same frying pan, add mushrooms and thyme; cook, stirring, until mushrooms are tender and liquid has almost evaporated. Season to taste.
3 Combine mushrooms, mesclun and pancetta in large bowl; toss gently. Serve topped with cheese.

prep + cook time 10 minutes **serves** 4
nutritional count per serving 19.9g total fat (6g saturated fat); 1066kJ (255 cal); 3.1g carbohydrate; 14.6g protein; 3.8g fibre

antipasto salad with minted yogurt

¼ cup coarsely chopped fresh mint

1 clove garlic, crushed

¾ cup (200g) greek-style yogurt

270g (9 ounces) bottled char-grilled antipasto, drained, chopped coarsely

310g (10 ounces) canned chickpeas (garbanzos), rinsed, drained

100g (3 ounces) mesclun

1 Combine mint, garlic and yogurt in small bowl.

2 Combine antipasto, chickpeas and mesclun in large bowl; toss gently.

3 Serve salad drizzled with minted yogurt.

prep time 10 minutes **serves** 4

nutritional count per serving 4.2g total fat (1.5g saturated fat); 631kJ (151 cal); 16.4g carbohydrate; 8.5g protein; 6.4g fibre

roasted capsicum and ricotta salad

2 medium orange capsicum (bell peppers) (400g)
2 medium red capsicum (bell peppers) (400g)
2 medium yellow capsicum (bell peppers) (400g)
2 medium green capsicum (bell peppers) (400g)
80g baby rocket leaves (arugula)
1 small red onion (100g), sliced thinly
1 cup (240g) ricotta cheese, crumbled

OREGANO VINAIGRETTE
⅓ cup (80ml) olive oil
2 tablespoons red wine vinegar
1 clove garlic, crushed
1 tablespoon finely chopped fresh oregano

1 Preheat oven to 200°C/400°F.
2 Quarter capsicums; discard seeds and membranes. Place, skin-side up, on oven tray. Roast, uncovered, about 20 minutes or until skin blisters and blackens. Cover capsicum pieces with plastic or paper for 5 minutes; peel away skin, then slice capsicum thickly.
3 Make oregano vinaigrette.
4 Combine capsicum, rocket and onion in large bowl; sprinkle with cheese, drizzle with vinaigrette.

OREGANO VINAIGRETTE Combine ingredients in screw-top jar; shake well.

prep + cook time 30 minutes **serves** 4
nutritional count per serving 25.6g total fat (6.9g saturated fat); 1396kJ (334 cal); 12.4g carbohydrate; 12.3g protein; 3.9g fibre

bean salad with creamy basil dressing

400g (12½ ounces) canned butter beans,
  rinsed, drained
400g (12½ ounces) canned borlotti beans,
  rinsed, drained
250g (8 ounces) cherry tomatoes, quartered
12 cherry bocconcini cheese (180g), halved
60g (2 ounces) baby rocket leaves (arugula)
½ cup (80g) roasted pine nuts

CREAMY BASIL DRESSING
2 tablespoons olive oil
2 tablespoons white wine vinegar
2 teaspoons white balsamic vinegar
2 tablespoons coarsely chopped fresh basil
¼ cup (60ml) pouring cream

1 Make creamy basil dressing.
2 Combine salad ingredients with dressing
in large bowl.

CREAMY BASIL DRESSING Combine oil,
vinegars and basil in small bowl. Add cream;
whisk until combined.

prep time 15 minutes serves 4
nutritional count per serving 37.1g total fat
(11g saturated fat); 1944kJ (465 cal);
13g carbohydrate; 17.1g protein; 7.7g fibre

chorizo, roasted capsicum and artichoke salad

2 large red capsicum (bell peppers) (700g)
2 cured chorizo sausages (340g), sliced thinly
280g (9 ounce) jar artichoke hearts in brine,
    drained, halved
200g (6½ ounces) red grape tomatoes, halved
80g (2½ ounces) curly endive leaves
½ cup firmly packed fresh flat-leaf parsley leaves

HERB AND GARLIC DRESSING
2 tablespoons olive oil
2 tablespoons white wine vinegar
1 tablespoon lemon juice
1 tablespoon finely chopped fresh basil
1 tablespoon finely chopped fresh oregano
2 cloves garlic, chopped finely

1 Preheat grill (broiler) to hot. Quarter capsicum;
discard seeds and membranes. Roast capsicum
under grill, skin-side up, until skin blisters and
blackens. Cover capsicum pieces with plastic or
paper for 5 minutes; peel away skin then cut pieces
in half diagonally.
2 Meanwhile, cook chorizo in large frying pan
until browned. Drain on absorbent paper.
3 Make herb and garlic dressing.
4 Combine capsicum, chorizo, dressing and
remaining ingredients in large bowl.

HERB AND GARLIC DRESSING Combine
ingredients in small bowl.

prep + cook time 25 minutes serves 4
nutritional count per serving 36g total fat
(10.8g saturated fat); 1885kJ (451 cal);
16.4g carbohydrate; 20.5g protein; 3.9g fibre

beef fillet with warm tomato, pesto and olive pasta

⅓ cup (80ml) olive oil
600g (1¼-pound) piece beef eye fillet
250g (8 ounces) cherry tomatoes, halved
500g (1 pound) farfalle pasta
⅔ cup (80g) seeded black olives
¼ cup (65g) basil pesto
2 teaspoons finely grated lemon rind
1 cup loosely packed fresh basil leaves, torn
1 cup (200g) ricotta cheese, crumbled

1 Heat 1 tablespoon of the oil in large frying pan; cook beef until cooked as desired. Remove from pan; cover to keep warm. Add tomato to same pan; cook, stirring occasionally, until just softened.
2 Meanwhile, cook pasta in large saucepan of boiling water until just tender; drain.

3 Combine pasta and tomato in large bowl with remaining oil, olives, pesto, rind and basil; toss gently.
4 Slice beef thickly; serve pasta mixture topped with beef and cheese.

prep + cook time 35 minutes **serves** 6
nutritional count per serving 28.7g total fat (7.5g saturated fat); 2721kJ (651 cal); 60.8g carbohydrate; 35.1g protein; 4g fibre

note Farfalle, the Italian pasta known in English as butterflies or bow ties, is good to use in dishes such as this because they help hold the other ingredients. You can replace farfalle with penne or spirals.

You need one large barbecued chicken, weighing approximately 900g (1¾ pounds), for this recipe.

chicken and rocket pesto pasta salad

375g (12 ounces) large shell pasta
1 cup (120g) frozen peas
3 cups (480g) shredded barbecued chicken
40g (1½ ounces) baby rocket leaves (arugula)

ROCKET PESTO
40g (1½ ounces) baby rocket leaves (arugula)
2 tablespoons pine nuts, roasted
½ cup (40g) finely grated parmesan cheese
2 teaspoons finely grated lemon rind
1 tablespoon lemon juice
¼ cup (60ml) olive oil

1 Cook pasta in large saucepan of boiling water until tender. Add peas during last 2 minutes of pasta cooking time; drain.
2 Meanwhile, make rocket pesto.
3 Combine pasta, peas and rocket pesto in large bowl with remaining ingredients.

ROCKET PESTO Blend or process rocket, nuts, cheese, rind and juice until finely chopped. With motor operating, gradually add oil in a thin steady stream; blend until pesto is smooth.

prep + cook time 30 minutes **serves** 4
nutritional count per serving 32.4g total fat (7.1g saturated fat); 3168kJ (758 cal); 66.6g carbohydrate; 47g protein; 5.6g fibre

tomato, mozzarella and prosciutto salad

3 slices prosciutto (45g)
3 large egg (plum) tomatoes (270g),
  chopped coarsely
300g (9½ ounces) cherry bocconcini cheese,
  chopped coarsely
1 medium avocado (250g), chopped coarsely
125g (4 ounces) mesclun
2 tablespoons olive oil

1   Cook prosciutto in heated medium frying pan
until crisp; drain on absorbent paper. When cool
enough to handle, break into pieces.
2   Combine prosciutto, tomato, cheese, avocado
and mesclun in serving bowl. Drizzle with oil;
season to taste.

prep + cook time 10 minutes **serves** 4
nutritional count per serving 31.2g total fat
(11.2g saturated fat); 1488kJ (356 cal);
1.8g carbohydrate; 16.9g protein; 2.1g fibre

seafood salads

prawn, crab and avocado salad

24 cooked medium king prawns (shrimp) (1kg)
8 large butter (boston) lettuce leaves
250g (8 ounces) crab meat, shredded coarsely
1 large avocado (320g), sliced thinly

THOUSAND ISLAND DRESSING
½ cup (150g) mayonnaise
1 tablespoon tomato sauce (ketchup)
½ small red capsicum (bell pepper) (75g),
 chopped finely
½ small white onion (40g), grated finely
8 pimiento-stuffed green olives, chopped finely
1 teaspoon lemon juice

1 Make thousand island dressing.
2 Shell and devein prawns, leaving tails intact.
3 Divide lettuce leaves among serving plates;
divide prawns, crab and avocado among lettuce
leaves. Drizzle with dressing.

THOUSAND ISLAND DRESSING Combine
ingredients in small bowl.

prep time 25 minutes serves 4
nutritional count per serving 26.6g total fat
(4.5g saturated fat); 1793kJ (429 cal);
10.9g carbohydrate; 35.6g protein; 2.5g fibre

Good quality frozen crab meat is available from fishmongers.

garlic prawn and noodle salad

750g (1½ pounds) uncooked medium king prawns
  (shrimp)
2 cloves garlic, crushed
125g (4 ounces) rice vermicelli
1 medium lemon (140g)
155g (5 ounces) snow peas, sliced thinly lengthways
⅓ cup finely chopped fresh mint

1 Shell and devein prawns, leaving tails intact.
Combine prawns and garlic in medium bowl.
Cook prawns on heated oiled grill plate (or grill
or barbecue) until changed in colour.
2 Meanwhile, place vermicelli in medium heatproof
bowl, cover with boiling water; stand until vermicelli
is tender, drain.
3 Finely grate 2 teaspoons rind from lemon. Squeeze
juice from lemon (you need 2 tablespoons juice).
4 Combine prawns, noodles, rind, juice, peas
and mint in large bowl; season to taste.

prep + cook time 25 minutes **serves** 4
nutritional count per serving 0.9g total fat
(0.1g saturated fat); 564kJ (135 cal);
9.2g carbohydrate; 21.3g protein; 1.7g fibre

grilled balmain bug salad

2 baby eggplants (120g)
1 medium zucchini (120g)
1 medium red capsicum (bell pepper) (200g), chopped finely
3 flat mushrooms (240g), quartered
2 tablespoons olive oil
6 uncooked balmain bug (rock lobster) tails (1.5kg), halved lengthways
250g (8 ounces) rocket (arugula)

CHILLI LIME BUTTER
60g (2 ounces) butter, softened
2 teaspoons finely grated lime rind
2 tablespoons lime juice
1 fresh long red chilli, chopped finely
2 cloves garlic, crushed

1 Using vegetable peeler, cut eggplant and zucchini into long, thin strips. Combine eggplant, zucchini, capsicum, mushrooms and oil in large bowl.

2 Cook vegetables, in batches, on heated oiled grill plate (or grill or barbecue) until tender. Cover to keep warm.
3 Cook balmain bug on heated oiled grill plate until cooked.
4 Meanwhile, make chilli lime butter.
5 Combine vegetables, balmain bug and chilli lime butter in large bowl.
6 Divide rocket among serving plates; top with vegetable and balmain bug mixture.

CHILLI LIME BUTTER Combine ingredients in small bowl.

prep + cook time 40 minutes serves 4
nutritional count per serving 25.1g total fat (10g saturated fat); 2282kJ (456 cal); 5.4g carbohydrate; 72.4g protein; 4.6g fibre

note Prawns (shrimp) or crabs can be used instead of balmain bugs.

char-grilled chilli squid and rice noodle salad

800g (1½ pounds) cleaned squid hoods
450g (14½ ounces) fresh wide rice noodles
1 medium red capsicum (bell pepper) (200g),
  sliced thinly
150g (4½ ounces) snow peas, halved
1 lebanese cucumber (130g), seeded, sliced thinly
1 small red onion (100g), sliced thinly
1 cup loosely packed fresh coriander leaves
  (cilantro)
⅓ cup coarsely chopped fresh mint

SWEET CHILLI DRESSING
½ cup (125ml) water
⅓ cup (75g) caster (superfine) sugar
1 tablespoon white vinegar
2 fresh small red thai (serrano) chillies,
  chopped finely

1 Cut squid down centre to open out; score
the inside in a diagonal pattern. Halve squid
lengthways; cut squid into 3cm (1¼ inch) pieces.
2 Make sweet chilli dressing.
3 Cook squid on heated oiled grill plate (or grill or
barbecue), in batches, until tender and browned.
4 Place noodles in large heatproof bowl, cover
with boiling water; separate with fork, drain.
Combine noodles in large serving bowl with squid,
dressing and remaining ingredients.

SWEET CHILLI DRESSING Stir the water and
sugar in small saucepan, over low heat, until sugar
dissolves; bring to the boil. Reduce heat; simmer,
uncovered, without stirring, about 5 minutes or
until syrup thickens slightly. Stir in vinegar and
chilli off the heat.

prep + cook time 30 minutes **serves** 4
nutritional count per serving 3.1g total fat
(0.8g saturated fat); 1584kJ (379 cal);
48.3g carbohydrate; 38.1g protein; 2.8g fibre

tuna salad

¼ cup (60ml) olive oil
2 tablespoons white wine vinegar
1 tablespoon lemon juice
2 teaspoons finely chopped fresh basil
2 teaspoons finely chopped fresh oregano
1 clove garlic, crushed
1 fresh long red chilli, chopped finely
1 medium iceberg lettuce, cut into wedges
425g (13½ ounces) canned tuna in springwater,
  drained, flaked
250g (8 ounces) cherry tomatoes, halved
1 medium avocado (250g), chopped coarsely
1 lebanese cucumber (130g), sliced thinly
1 small red onion (100g), sliced thinly

1 Combine oil, vinegar, juice, herbs, garlic and
chilli in screw-top jar; shake well.
2 Place lettuce wedges on serving plate; top with
remaining ingredients. Drizzle with dressing.

prep time 15 minutes **serves** 4
nutritional count per serving 26.1g total fat
(4.9g saturated fat); 1492kJ (357 cal);
4.6g carbohydrate; 24.4g protein; 4.9g fibre

Feel free to pick and choose any vegies to toss into this salad;
capsicum (bell pepper) and radish would taste great, too.
A can of salmon can be substituted for the tuna.

prawn and mango salad

1kg (2 pounds) cooked medium king prawns
 (shrimp)
1 medium mango (430g), sliced thinly
2 baby cos lettuce, leaves separated
¼ cup coarsely chopped fresh chives
2 tablespoons olive oil
1 tablespoon white balsamic vinegar

1 Shell and devein prawns, leaving tails intact.
2 Combine prawns and remaining ingredients in large bowl.

prep time 25 minutes **serves** 4
nutritional count per serving 10.3g total fat
(1.4g saturated fat); 1066kJ (255 cal);
11.3g carbohydrate; 27.7g protein; 3.1g fibre

note To save time, buy shelled prawns from the fishmonger.
White balsamic vinegar is available from most major supermarkets. Use white wine vinegar if you prefer.

tuna tartare on baby cos

200g (6½-ounce) piece sashimi tuna, trimmed
1 tablespoon rinsed, drained capers,
  chopped finely
2 teaspoons prepared horseradish
⅓ cup (80ml) lime juice
2 small tomatoes (180g), seeded, chopped finely
1 small avocado (200g), chopped finely
1 small red onion (100g), chopped finely
1 baby cos lettuce, leaves separated
1 tablespoon extra virgin olive oil

1 Cut tuna into 5mm (¼ inch) pieces; combine
in medium bowl with capers, horseradish and
1 tablespoon of the juice. Cover; refrigerate
30 minutes.

2 Combine tomato, avocado, onion and remaining
juice in medium bowl.
3 Serve lettuce leaves topped with tomato mixture
and tuna tartare; drizzle with oil.

prep time 25 minutes (+ refrigeration) serves 6
nutritional count per serving 10.4g total fat
(2.3g saturated fat); 610kJ (146 cal);
2.4g carbohydrate; 9.8g protein; 1.6g fibre

note Tuna sold as sashimi has to meet stringent
guidelines regarding its handling and treatment
after leaving the water. It is a good idea to buy it
only from a fishmonger you trust, or to seek advice
from local authorities before eating any raw seafood.

warm salad of smoked salmon, spinach and potato

400g (12½ ounces) baby new potatoes, quartered
2 tablespoons pouring cream
¼ cup (75g) mayonnaise
2 tablespoons finely chopped fresh dill
100g (3 ounces) baby spinach leaves
200g (6½ ounces) sliced smoked salmon,
  chopped coarsely

1 Boil, steam or microwave potato until tender; drain. Cover to keep warm.
2 Meanwhile, make dressing by combining cream, mayonnaise and dill in small bowl.
3 Place warm potatoes in large bowl; season. Add spinach and salmon; stir gently.
4 Divide salad between serving plates; drizzle with dressing.

prep + cook time 15 minutes **serves** 4
nutritional count per serving 12.8g total fat
(4g saturated fat); 1037kJ (248 cal);
17.1g carbohydrate; 14.8g protein; 2.8g fibre

smoked trout and potato salad

750g (1½ pounds) baby new potatoes, halved
2 x 385g (12 ounce) whole smoked trout
2 tablespoons lemon juice
1 tablespoon olive oil
1 teaspoon dijon mustard
1 small red onion (100g), sliced thinly
2 green onions (scallions), sliced thinly
2 tablespoons rinsed, drained capers
1 tablespoon finely chopped fresh dill
4 large iceberg lettuce leaves

1 Boil, steam or microwave potato until tender; drain. Cook potato on heated oiled grill plate (or grill or barbecue) until browned both sides.
2 Meanwhile, discard skin and bones from fish; flake flesh into large bowl.
3 Make dressing by combining juice, oil and mustard in screw-top jar; shake well.
4 Combine potato, dressing, onions, capers and dill in bowl with trout; divide salad among lettuce leaves.

prep + cook time 35 minutes **serves** 4
nutritional count per serving 16.6g total fat (1.9g saturated fat); 1404kJ (336 cal); 27.6g carbohydrate; 31.2g protein; 4.8g fibre

warm squid and tomato salad

1 cup (120g) seeded black olives, chopped coarsely
400g (12½ ounces) fetta cheese, crumbled
1 tablespoon finely grated lemon rind
½ cup loosely packed fresh oregano leaves
12 cleaned small squid hoods (700g)
4 medium egg (plum) tomatoes (300g), quartered
1 large red onion (300g), cut into wedges
2 tablespoons olive oil
1 baby endive (300g), trimmed

OREGANO AND RED WINE DRESSING
¼ cup (60ml) olive oil
2 tablespoons red wine vinegar
1 clove garlic, crushed
1 tablespoon finely chopped fresh oregano

1   Preheat oven to 180°C/350°F.
2   Combine olives, cheese, rind and oregano in
small bowl; push cheese mixture into squid hoods.
Secure with toothpicks; refrigerate until required.

3   Place tomato and onion in large baking dish;
drizzle with oil. Roast about 15 minutes or until
tomato begins to soften. Remove dish from oven.
Place squid on top of tomato mixture. Roast about
10 minutes or until squid are cooked through.
4   Meanwhile, make oregano and red wine dressing.
5   Combine tomato, onion and endive in large
bowl; divide salad among serving plates. Top with
squid; drizzle with dressing.

OREGANO AND RED WINE DRESSING Combine
ingredients in screw-top jar; shake well.

prep + cook time 45 minutes serves 4
nutritional count per serving 48.8g total fat
(19.3g saturated fat); 2913kJ (697 cal);
13.2g carbohydrate; 50.2g protein; 4.3g fibre

salt and pepper baby octopus with aïoli

500g (1 pound) cleaned baby octopus,
  halved lengthways
2 teaspoons sea salt
3 teaspoons cracked black pepper
150g (4½ ounces) mesclun
1 lebanese cucumber (130g), sliced thinly
125g (4 ounces) cherry tomatoes, halved
2 tablespoons olive oil

AÏOLI
1 egg yolk
1 clove garlic, crushed
1 teaspoon dijon mustard
1 tablespoon white wine vinegar
1 cup (250ml) olive oil
1 teaspoon lemon juice

LEMON DRESSING
1 tablespoon lemon juice
1 tablespoon olive oil

1 Make aïoli.
2 Combine octopus, salt and pepper in medium bowl.
3 Make lemon dressing.
4 Place mesclun, cucumber, tomato and dressing in large bowl; toss gently to combine.
5 Heat oil in wok; stir-fry octopus, in batches, until browned lightly and cooked through.
6 Serve octopus on salad; accompany with aïoli, and lemon wedges, if you like.

AÏOLI Blend or process egg yolk, garlic, mustard and vinegar until combined. With motor operating, gradually add oil in a thin, steady stream; process until aïoli thickens slightly. Stir in juice.

LEMON DRESSING Place ingredients in screw-top jar; shake well.

prep + cook time 20 minutes **serves** 4
nutritional count per serving 74.3g total fat (10.9g saturated fat); 3348kJ (801 cal); 3.5g carbohydrate; 31.4g protein; 2.1g fibre

warm salmon and lemon-herbed pasta salad

1 cup (120g) frozen peas
170g (5½ ounces) asparagus, trimmed,
  chopped coarsely
500g (1-pound) piece salmon fillet
625g (1¼ pounds) spinach and ricotta agnolotti
½ cup firmly packed fresh flat-leaf parsley leaves
1 tablespoon water
¼ cup (60ml) olive oil
1 teaspoon finely grated lemon rind
¼ cup (60ml) lemon juice

1 Boil, steam or microwave peas and asparagus,
separately, until just tender; drain. Rinse under cold
water; drain.
2 Cook fish on heated oiled grill plate (or grill or
barbecue) until browned both sides and cooked
as desired. Place fish in large bowl then, using fork,
flake into chunks.
3 Meanwhile, cook pasta in large saucepan
of boiling water until just tender; drain. Place
in bowl with fish.
4 Combine parsley, the water, oil, rind and juice in
small jug; pour into bowl with fish. Add peas and
asparagus; toss salad gently to combine.

prep + cook time 35 minutes **serves** 4
nutritional count per serving 33.7g total fat
(10.6g saturated fat); 2428kJ (581 cal);
26.9g carbohydrate; 39.8g protein; 5.5g fibre

Fresh spinach and ricotta agnolotti is found in most supermarkets'
refrigerated sections. You can substitute ravioli or tortellini for the
agnolotti, but none should contain meat or poultry in their filling.

char-grilled octopus salad

1 fresh long red chilli, chopped finely
1 teaspoon finely grated lime rind
1 teaspoon salt
2 tablespoons rice flour
1kg (2 pounds) cleaned octopus, quartered
200g (6½ ounces) mizuna
150g (4½ ounces) snow peas, sliced thinly

CHILLI LIME DRESSING
1 fresh small red thai (serrano) chilli, chopped finely
1 teaspoon finely grated lime rind
2 tablespoons lime juice
1 tablespoon peanut oil
2cm (¾ inch) piece fresh ginger (10g), grated

1 Combine chilli, rind, salt and flour in large bowl;
add octopus, toss to coat in mixture.
2 Make chilli lime dressing.
3 Cook octopus on heated oiled grill plate (or grill
or barbecue) about 20 minutes or until tender.
4 Combine remaining ingredients in large bowl
with octopus and dressing.

CHILLI LIME DRESSING Combine ingredients
in screw-top jar; shake well.

prep + cook time 40 minutes **serves** 4
nutritional count per serving 9.4g total fat
(1.8g saturated fat); 1668kJ (399 cal);
10.5g carbohydrate; 65.8g protein; 2.2g fibre

poultry salads

creamy chicken and pasta salad

3 cups (750ml) water
400g (12½ ounces) chicken breast fillets
500g (1 pound) large shell pasta
2 celery stalks (300g), trimmed, sliced thinly
1 small red onion (100g), sliced thinly
1 cup (120g) roasted pecans
½ cup (90g) thinly sliced dill pickles
60g (2 ounces) baby rocket leaves (arugula)

CREAMY TARRAGON DRESSING
¾ cup (225g) mayonnaise
½ cup (120g) sour cream
2 tablespoons lemon juice
1 tablespoon finely chopped fresh tarragon

1 Bring the water to the boil in medium saucepan, add chicken; simmer, covered, about 10 minutes. Cool chicken in poaching liquid 10 minutes; drain, slice thinly.
2 Meanwhile, cook pasta in large saucepan of boiling water until tender; drain. Rinse under cold water; drain.
3 Make creamy tarragon dressing.
4 Combine pasta in large bowl with chicken, dressing and remaining ingredients.

CREAMY TARRAGON DRESSING Combine ingredients in small bowl.

prep + cook time 35 minutes serves 6
nutritional count per serving 39.1g total fat (8.8g saturated fat); 3097kJ (741 cal); 67.5g carbohydrate; 27.1g protein; 5.7g fibre

note Cornichon, French for gherkin, is a very small variety of pickled cucumber; it can be used in place of the dill pickles.

chicken, pomegranate and burghul salad

¼ cup (60ml) olive oil
¼ cup (60ml) pomegranate molasses
1 tablespoon ground cumin
2 cloves garlic, crushed
1kg (2 pounds) chicken breast fillets
1½ cups (375ml) chicken stock
1½ cups (240g) burghul
1 cup (250ml) pomegranate pulp
1 medium red onion (170g), sliced thinly
3 cups (350g) firmly packed trimmed watercress
2 cups firmly packed fresh flat-leaf parsley leaves
1 cup (110g) coarsely chopped roasted walnuts
150g (4½ ounce) fetta cheese, crumbled

POMEGRANATE DRESSING
¼ cup (60ml) olive oil
¼ cup (60ml) lemon juice
3 teaspoons honey
3 teaspoons pomegranate molasses

1 Combine oil, molasses, cumin and garlic in large bowl with chicken. Cover; refrigerate 3 hours or overnight.
2 Bring stock to the boil in medium saucepan. Remove from heat, add burghul; cover, stand 5 minutes.
3 Meanwhile, make pomegranate dressing.
4 Drain chicken, discard marinade. Cook chicken on heated oiled grill plate (or grill or barbecue), until browned and cooked through. Cover chicken; stand 10 minutes, then slice thickly.
5 Combine chicken, burghul and remaining ingredients with dressing in large bowl; divide among serving plates.

POMEGRANATE DRESSING Combine ingredients in screw-top jar; shake well.

prep + cook time 45 minutes (+ refrigeration)
serves 6
nutritional count per serving 47.1g total fat (10.3g saturated fat); 3503kJ (838 cal); 47.6g carbohydrate; 50.2g protein; 13.1g fibre

You need one large pomegranate to get the amount of pulp required for this recipe. To remove the pulp, cut it in half, then hit the shell with a wooden spoon – the seeds usually fall out easily; it they don't, dig them out with a spoon.
Pomegranate molasses is available at Middle-Eastern food stores, specialty food shops and some delicatessens.
If you're short on time, it's fine to skip the marinating, just make sure the chicken is well-coated with the oil mixture.

duck, pear and blue cheese salad

4 duck breast fillets (600g)
1 small red oakleaf lettuce, leaves separated
2 witlof (belgian endive) (250g), leaves separated
1 medium pear (230g), halved, cored, sliced thinly
1 cup (100g) roasted walnuts
150g (4½ ounces) soft blue cheese, crumbled

RED WINE VINAIGRETTE
¼ cup (60ml) olive oil
¼ cup (60ml) red wine vinegar
2 teaspoons wholegrain mustard

1 Cook duck, skin-side down, in heated large frying pan about 5 minutes or until skin is browned and crisp. Turn duck; cook about 5 minutes or until cooked as desired. Drain on absorbent paper; slice thinly.
2 Meanwhile, make red wine vinaigrette.
3 Combine duck, lettuce, witlof, pear and nuts in large bowl; drizzle with vinaigrette, sprinkle with cheese.

RED WINE VINAIGRETTE Combine ingredients in screw-top jar; shake well.

prep + cook time 25 minutes serves 4
nutritional count per serving 99g total fat
(27.5g saturated fat); 4431kJ (1060 cal);
8.8g carbohydrate; 33.1g protein; 6.5g fibre

sesame chicken and honey soy dressing

600g (1¼ pounds) chicken breast fillets,
  halved lengthways
1 egg white, beaten lightly
½ cup (75g) sesame seeds
2 tablespoons olive oil
100g (3 ounces) mixed baby asian greens
1 small red onion (100g), sliced thinly
⅔ cup (100g) coarsely chopped roasted
  unsalted cashew nuts

HONEY SOY DRESSING
¼ cup (60ml) lemon juice
2 tablespoons light soy sauce
1 tablespoon olive oil
2 teaspoons honey
½ teaspoon sesame oil

1 Dip chicken in egg white, then coat in sesame
seeds. Heat oil in large frying pan; cook chicken
until cooked through. Cover chicken; stand
5 minutes then slice thickly.
2 Meanwhile, make honey soy dressing.
3 Combine greens, onion and nuts in medium
bowl; divide among serving plates, top with
chicken, drizzle with dressing.

HONEY SOY DRESSING Combine ingredients
in small bowl.

prep + cook time 25 minutes **serves** 4
nutritional count per serving 45.9g total fat
(8g saturated fat); 2638kJ (631 cal);
11.8g carbohydrate; 42.1g protein; 3.8g fibre

Pappadums, dried cracker-like wafers made from lentil and rice flours, must be reconstituted before they are eaten. We do this the low-fat way, giving them a burst in a microwave oven, but they are usually deep-fried to make them puff up and double in size. We used large plain pappadums here, but there are many sizes and flavour combinations to choose from.

tandoori chicken, spinach and mint salad with spiced yogurt

⅓ cup (100g) tandoori paste
¼ cup (70g) yogurt
800g (1½ pounds) chicken tenderloins
1 tablespoon vegetable oil
8 large uncooked pappadums
150g (4½ ounces) baby spinach leaves
2 lebanese cucumbers (260g), sliced thickly
250g (8 ounces) cherry tomatoes, halved
1 cup firmly packed fresh mint leaves

SPICED YOGURT
1 clove garlic, crushed
¾ cup (210g) yogurt
1 tablespoon lemon juice
1 teaspoon ground cumin
1 teaspoon ground coriander

1 Combine paste and yogurt in medium bowl with chicken. Cover; refrigerate 3 hours or overnight.
2 Make spiced yogurt.
3 Heat oil in large frying pan; cook chicken, in batches, until cooked through.
4 Microwave 2 pappadums at a time on HIGH (100%) about 30 seconds.
5 Combine chicken in large bowl with spinach, cucumber, tomato and mint. Drizzle with yogurt; serve with pappadums.

SPICED YOGURT Combine ingredients in small jug.

prep + cook time 35 minutes (+ refrigeration)
serves 4
nutritional count per serving 12.5g total fat
(3.4g saturated fat); 1731kJ (414 cal);
16.4g carbohydrate; 55.1g protein; 6.7g fibre

chicken, roasted kumara, cranberry and spinach salad

1 large kumara (orange sweet potato) (500g),
  cut into 2cm (¾ inch) pieces
1 medium red onion (170g), cut into wedges
1 tablespoon maple syrup
1 tablespoon olive oil
600g (1¼ pounds) chicken breast fillets
90g (3 ounces) baby spinach leaves
⅓ cup (45g) dried cranberries
⅓ cup (50g) pine nuts

CRANBERRY DRESSING
2 tablespoons olive oil
¼ cup (80g) whole berry cranberry sauce, warmed
1 tablespoon red wine vinegar

1 Preheat oven to 220°C/425°F.
2 Combine kumara, onion, syrup and oil in large shallow baking dish; roast about 35 minutes or until vegetables are tender, stirring halfway through roasting time.
3 Meanwhile, make cranberry dressing.
4 Cook chicken in heated oiled medium frying pan until cooked through. Remove from pan; slice thickly.
5 Combine kumara mixture, half the dressing, chicken, spinach, cranberries and nuts in medium bowl. Divide salad among serving plates; drizzle with remaining dressing.

CRANBERRY DRESSING Whisk ingredients in small jug to combine.

prep + cook time 45 minutes serves 4
nutritional count per serving 30.9g total fat
(5g saturated fat); 2449kJ (586 cal);
37.7g carbohydrate; 37.2g protein; 4.3g fibre

smoked chicken chow-mein salad with raspberry macadamia dressing

100g (3 ounce) packet fried noodles
½ cup (70g) roasted macadamias, chopped coarsely
100g (3 ounces) baby rocket leaves (arugula)
100g (3 ounces) mizuna
1 small red onion (100g), sliced thinly
½ cup firmly packed fresh flat-leaf parsley leaves
½ cup firmly packed fresh mint leaves
800g (1½ pounds) smoked chicken breast fillets,
  sliced thinly

RASPBERRY MACADAMIA DRESSING
2 cloves garlic, crushed
¼ cup (60ml) raspberry vinegar
1 tablespoon wholegrain mustard
⅓ cup (80ml) macadamia oil

1 Combine ingredients for raspberry macadamia dressing in screw-top jar; shake well.
2 Combine salad ingredients in large bowl with dressing; toss gently.

prep time 20 minutes **serves** 6
nutritional count per serving 32.3g total fat (6.3g saturated fat); 1923kJ (460 cal); 5.8g carbohydrate; 35.5g protein; 2.8g fibre

duck salad with mandarin and pomegranate

150g (4½ ounces) sugar snap peas
1kg (2-pound) chinese barbecued duck
2 small mandarins (200g), segmented
1 red mignonette lettuce (280g), leaves separated
⅓ cup (60g) pomegranate pulp
¾ cup (120g) roasted slivered almonds

LEMON DIJON DRESSING
1 clove garlic, crushed
1 teaspoon dijon mustard
2 tablespoons lemon juice
2 tablespoons olive oil

1 Boil, steam or microwave peas until just tender; drain. Rinse under cold water; drain.
2 Remove meat, leaving skin on, from duck; discard bones. Chop meat coarsely; place in large bowl with peas, mandarin, lettuce, pomegranate and nuts.
3 Make lemon dijon dressing. Pour dressing over salad; toss gently to combine.

LEMON DIJON DRESSING Combine ingredients in screw-top jar; shake well.

prep + cook time 35 minutes serves 4
nutritional count per serving 58.3g total fat (12.7g saturated fat); 2876kJ (688 cal); 8.9g carbohydrate; 33.3g protein; 6.5g fibre

tip You need one large pomegranate for this recipe.

turkey, cranberry and peanut salad in butter lettuce leaves

1.5kg (3-pound) boneless turkey breast
1.5 litres (6 cups) water
½ cup (125ml) red wine vinegar
1 teaspoon dijon mustard
¼ cup (60ml) light olive oil
⅔ cup (90g) dried cranberries
3 celery stalks (450g), trimmed, sliced thinly
1¼ cups (100g) bean sprouts
1 cup (50g) snow pea sprouts
½ cup (70g) roasted unsalted peanuts
½ cup firmly packed fresh mint leaves, torn
1 butter (boston) lettuce, leaves separated

1 Cut turkey into three equal-sized pieces. Bring the water to the boil in large saucepan; add turkey. Simmer, covered, about 35 minutes or until turkey is cooked. Cool turkey in poaching liquid 15 minutes. Drain turkey; shred coarsely.

2 Combine vinegar, mustard and oil in large bowl. Add turkey, cranberries, celery, sprouts, nuts and mint; toss gently. Serve salad in lettuce leaves.

prep + cook time 1 hour (+ cooling) **serves** 6
nutritional count per serving 23.1g total fat
(4.1g saturated fat); 2019kJ (483 cal);
6.7g carbohydrate; 59.7g protein; 4.2g fibre

warm duck, apple and walnut salad

2 large green-skinned apples (400g) unpeeled,
   quartered, cored
¾ cup (180ml) cider vinegar
¾ cup (180ml) water
1 tablespoon light brown sugar
2 x 5cm (2 inch) strips lemon rind
1 cinnamon stick
1 star anise
4 duck breast fillets (600g), skin on
1 teaspoon sea salt flakes
1 teaspoon ground sichuan pepper
¼ teaspoon ground ginger
45g (1½ ounces) butter
90g (3 ounces) baby spinach leaves
4 green onions (scallions), cut into
   3cm (1¼ inch) pieces
¼ cup (25g) coarsely chopped walnuts

SWEET MUSTARD DRESSING
2 tablespoons rice vinegar
1 tablespoon olive oil
2 teaspoons mirin
1 teaspoon dijon mustard

1 Combine apple, vinegar, the water, sugar, rind, cinnamon and star anise in medium saucepan; bring to the boil. Reduce heat; simmer, uncovered, about 8 minutes or until apple is tender. Drain; gently cut each apple in half lengthways. Refrigerate 20 minutes.
2 Meanwhile, make sweet mustard dressing.
3 Remove excess fat from duck; rub duck with combined salt, pepper and ginger. Prick duck skins with fork several times. Cook duck, skin-side down, in heated oiled large frying pan about 8 minutes or until crisp. Turn duck; cook about 5 minutes or until cooked as desired. Cover duck; stand 5 minutes then slice thinly.
4 Meanwhile, heat butter in medium frying pan; cook apple, turning occasionally, until caramelised.
5 Divide combined spinach and onion among serving plates; top with duck, apple and nuts, drizzle with dressing.

SWEET MUSTARD DRESSING Combine ingredients in screw-top jar; shake well.

prep + cook time 45 minutes (+ refrigeration)
serves 4
nutritional count per serving 72.6g total fat (23g saturated fat); 3290kJ (787 cal); 12.6g carbohydrate; 21.5g protein; 2.7g fibre

Refrigerating the apples after they've been cooked helps them to hold their shape.

turkey larb with sour cherries

1 tablespoon peanut oil
600g (1¼ pounds) minced (ground) turkey
2 cloves garlic, crushed
2cm (¾ inch) piece fresh ginger (10g), grated
1 fresh long red chilli, chopped finely
2 tablespoons light brown sugar
1 tablespoon fish sauce
1 tablespoon japanese soy sauce
2 tablespoons morello sour cherry syrup
1 cup (200g) drained, seeded bottled
   morello sour cherries
1 cup loosely packed fresh coriander leaves
   (cilantro)
8 medium cos lettuce leaves
½ cup (40g) bean sprouts

1 Heat oil in wok; stir-fry turkey, garlic, ginger and chilli until turkey changes colour. Remove from wok.
2 Add sugar, sauces and cherry syrup; bring to the boil. Reduce heat; simmer, uncovered, 2 minutes. Return turkey mixture to wok; cook, uncovered, about 2 minutes or until larb mixture is slightly dry and sticky. Add cherries; stir until hot. Remove from heat; stir in coriander.
3 Divide larb mixture among lettuce leaves; sprinkle with sprouts.

prep + cook time 30 minutes **serves** 4
nutritional count per serving 16.7g total fat (4.5g saturated fat); 1618kJ (387 cal); 26.7g carbohydrate; 30.9g protein; 2g fibre

tip Drain the morello sour cherries and reserve the syrup for use in the recipe.

char-grilled chicken, vegetables and haloumi salad

2 tablespoons olive oil
1 tablespoon balsamic vinegar
2 cloves garlic, crushed
1 tablespoon coarsely chopped fresh rosemary
800g (1½ pounds) chicken thigh fillets
600g (1¼-pound) piece pumpkin, sliced thinly
300g (9½ ounces) asparagus, trimmed
2 x 180g (5½ ounce) packets haloumi cheese
250g (8 ounces) rocket trimmed (arugula)

ROSEMARY BALSAMIC DRESSING
2 tablespoons olive oil
1 tablespoon balsamic vinegar
1 tablespoon lemon juice
1 tablespoon coarsely chopped fresh rosemary

1   Make rosemary balsamic dressing.
2   Combine oil, vinegar, garlic, rosemary and chicken in medium bowl. Cook chicken on heated oiled grill plate (or grill or barbecue). Cover chicken; stand 5 minutes then slice thickly.
3   Cook pumpkin and asparagus, in batches, on grill plate until tender. Transfer to large bowl; cover.
4   Slice cheese thickly; cook on cleaned grill plate until browned both sides.
5   Combine chicken, cheese, rocket and dressing in bowl with pumpkin and asparagus; toss gently.

ROSEMARY BALSAMIC DRESSING Combine ingredients in screw-top jar; shake well.

prep + cook time 50 minutes **serves** 4
nutritional count per serving 49.1g total fat (17.2g saturated fat); 3106kJ (743 cal); 12.2g carbohydrate; 62.6g protein; 3.8g fibre

meat salads

pork and beetroot salad

2 bunches baby beetroot (beets) (1kg)
2 bunches spring onions (800g)
2 tablespoons olive oil
750g (1½ pounds) pork fillets
150g (4½ ounces) mixed baby asian greens
1 cup (100g) coarsely chopped roasted walnuts

HORSERADISH DRESSING
¾ cup (180g) crème fraîche
3 teaspoons dijon mustard
3 teaspoons prepared horseradish
1 tablespoon lemon juice
2 tablespoons water

1 Preheat oven to 200°C/400°F.
2 Cut stalk and root ends of beetroot to 3cm (1¼ inch) lengths; halve beetroot lengthways. Trim roots from onions; trim stems to 5cm (2 inches). Halve onions lengthways. Place beetroot and onion, in single layer, in large shallow baking dish; drizzle with half the oil. Roast, uncovered, 30 minutes or until tender.
3 Meanwhile, heat remaining oil in large frying pan; cook pork until cooked as desired. Cover pork; stand 5 minutes then slice thickly.
4 Make horseradish dressing.
5 Divide asian greens among serving plates; top with roasted vegetables and sliced pork. Drizzle with dressing; sprinkle with nuts.

HORSERADISH DRESSING Whisk ingredients in small jug until smooth.

prep + cook time 50 minutes serves 6
nutritional count per serving 33.2g total fat (10.6g saturated fat); 2249kJ (538 cal); 20.5g carbohydrate; 35.8g protein; 8.8g fibre

Pomegranate molasses is available at Middle-Eastern food stores, specialty-food shops and some delicatessens.

lamb and lentil salad

1½ cups (300g) french-style green lentils
750g (1½ pounds) lamb backstraps
1 tablespoon olive oil
2 teaspoons ground cumin
350g (11 ounces) baby green beans
1 small red onion (100g), sliced thinly
1 cup (110g) coarsely chopped roasted walnuts
2 cups firmly packed fresh flat-leaf parsley leaves
200g (6½ ounce) fetta cheese, crumbled

POMEGRANATE DRESSING
⅓ cup (80ml) olive oil
2 tablespoons lemon juice
1 tablespoon pomegranate molasses
2 teaspoons light brown sugar

1 Cook lentils in large saucepan of boiling water, uncovered, about 15 minutes or until tender; drain.
2 Meanwhile, make pomegranate dressing. Combine half the dressing with lentils in large bowl.
3 Cook lamb on heated oiled grill plate (or grill or barbecue), brushing frequently with combined oil and cumin, until cooked as desired. Cover lamb; stand 5 minutes then slice thickly.
4 Boil, steam or microwave beans until tender; drain. Rinse under cold water; drain.
5 Add onion, nuts, parsley, cheese and remaining dressing to lentils; toss gently to combine. Serve lentil salad with lamb.

POMEGRANATE DRESSING Combine ingredients in screw-top jar; shake well.

prep + cook time 40 minutes serves 6
nutritional count per serving 41.3g total fat (10.2g saturated fat); 2880kJ (689 cal); 26.4g carbohydrate; 48.3g protein; 10.8g fibre

peppered lamb with watercress, pea and mint salad

2 tablespoons mixed peppercorns
1 tablespoon olive oil
600g (1¼ pounds) lamb fillets
1 cup (160g) fresh or frozen peas
250g (8 ounces) yellow teardrop tomatoes, halved
100g (3 ounces) trimmed watercress
200g (6½ ounces) fetta cheese, cut into thin strips
¼ cup coarsely chopped fresh mint

WHITE WINE VINAIGRETTE
¼ cup (60ml) white wine vinegar
1 tablespoon olive oil
1 clove garlic, crushed

1   Using mortar and pestle, crush peppercorns until ground coarsely. Combine ground peppercorns, oil and lamb in medium bowl. Cook lamb in heated oiled large frying pan until cooked as desired. Cover lamb; stand 5 minutes then slice thinly.
2   Meanwhile, make white wine vinaigrette.
3   Boil, steam or microwave peas until tender; drain. Rinse under cold water; drain.
4   Combine lamb, peas, vinaigrette and remaining ingredients in large bowl.

WHITE WINE VINAIGRETTE   Combine ingredients in screw-top jar; shake well.

prep + cook time 30 minutes serves 4
nutritional count per serving 31.1g total fat (12g saturated fat); 2006kJ (480 cal); 5.1g carbohydrate; 43.2g protein; 5g fibre

mexican beef salad

35g (1 ounce) packet taco seasoning mix
600g (1¼-pound) piece beef rump steak
420g (13½ ounces) canned four-bean mix,
   rinsed, drained
125g (4 ounces) canned corn kernels,
   rinsed, drained
2 large tomatoes (440g), chopped finely
½ cup coarsely chopped fresh coriander (cilantro)

1   Rub seasoning mix over both sides of steak. Cook steak in heated oiled large frying pan. Cover steak; stand 5 minutes then slice thickly.
2   Meanwhile, combine beans, corn, tomato and coriander in medium bowl. Divide salad between serving plates; top with steak. Serve with lime wedges, if you like.

prep + cook time 15 minutes **serves** 4
nutritional count per serving 10.7g total fat
(4.6g saturated fat); 1392kJ (333 cal);
15.9g carbohydrate; 39.8g protein; 6.6g fibre

cajun-spiced beef and garlicky bean salad

750g (1½-pound) piece beef fillet
1 tablespoon cajun spice mix
420g (13½ ounces) canned four-bean mix,
    rinsed, drained
2 lebanese cucumbers (260g), halved lengthways,
    sliced thinly
4 small tomatoes (360g), cut into wedges
1 medium red onion (170g), sliced thinly
1 medium avocado (250g), sliced thickly
½ cup finely chopped fresh coriander (cilantro)

GARLIC VINAIGRETTE
¼ cup (60ml) lemon juice
¼ cup (60ml) olive oil
2 cloves garlic, crushed

1 Make garlic vinaigrette.
2 Sprinkle beef both sides with spice mix; cook on
heated oiled grill plate (or grill or barbecue). Cover
beef; stand 5 minutes then slice thinly.
3 Combine remaining ingredients in large bowl with
dressing; toss gently. Serve salad topped with beef.

GARLIC VINAIGRETTE Combine ingredients in
small bowl.

prep + cook time 25 minutes serves 4
nutritional count per serving 5.3g total fat
(8.8g saturated fat); 2445kJ (585 cal);
16.3g carbohydrate; 47.5g protein; 7.5 g fibre

note Cajun spice mix, a blend of ground herbs and
spices that can include basil, paprika, tarragon,
fennel, thyme or cayenne, is available at most
supermarkets and speciality spice shops.

blt salad

250g (8 ounces) cherry tomatoes
cooking-oil spray
6 rindless bacon slices (390g)
1 small french stick (150g)
180g (5½ ounces) bocconcini cheese, halved
1 large cos lettuce, leaves separated, torn

MUSTARD MAYONNAISE
⅓ cup (100g) mayonnaise
2 teaspoons wholegrain mustard
¼ cup (60ml) lemon juice

1 Preheat grill (broiler). Make mustard mayonnaise.
2 Place tomatoes on oven tray; spray with oil. Grill
until softened slightly. Cover to keep warm.
3 Grill bacon until crisp. Chop coarsely.
4 Cut bread into 8 slices; toast under grill until
browned both sides.
5 Combine tomato, bacon, cheese and lettuce
in large bowl. Serve salad with toast; drizzle with
mustard mayonnaise.

MUSTARD MAYONNAISE Combine ingredients
in small bowl.

prep + cook time 25 minutes **serves** 4
nutritional count per serving 31.2g total fat
(16.4g saturated fat); 2312kJ (553 cal);
31.1g carbohydrate; 33.9g protein; 7.1g fibre

turkish lamb and yogurt salad

600g (1¼ pounds) lamb backstrap
2 tablespoons sumac
1 tablespoon olive oil
¼ cup (70g) yogurt
2 tablespoons lemon juice
250g (8 ounces) cherry tomatoes, halved
2 lebanese cucumbers (260g), seeded,
  sliced thinly
½ cup loosely packed fresh flat-leaf parsley leaves
½ cup loosely packed fresh mint leaves
1 small red onion (100g), sliced thinly

1 Rub lamb with sumac. Heat oil in large frying pan; cook lamb until cooked as desired. Cover lamb; stand 5 minutes then slice thinly.
2 Meanwhile, to make dressing, whisk yogurt and juice in small jug.
3 Combine lamb and remaining ingredients in large bowl; drizzle with dressing.

prep + cook time 25 minutes **serves** 4
nutritional count per serving 10.8g total fat
(3.4g saturated fat); 1062kJ (254 cal);
5.1g carbohydrate; 32.9g protein; 2.7g fibre

oven-roasted beef fillet and beetroot with horseradish crème fraîche

500g (1-pound) piece beef eye fillet, trimmed
2 tablespoons wholegrain mustard
1 tablespoon horseradish cream
2 tablespoons olive oil
1kg (2 pounds) baby beetroots (beets), trimmed
150g (4½ ounces) baby rocket leaves (arugula)
2 lebanese cucumbers (260g), sliced thinly
1 cup loosely packed fresh flat-leaf parsley leaves

PARMESAN CROÛTONS
1 small french stick (150g)
1 tablespoon olive oil
½ cup (40g) finely grated parmesan cheese

HORSERADISH CRÈME FRAÎCHE
¼ cup (60g) crème fraîche
2 tablespoons horseradish cream
1 tablespoon lemon juice

1 Preheat oven to 220°C/425°F.
2 Tie beef with kitchen string at 3cm (1¼ inch) intervals. Combine mustard, horseradish and oil in small jug; brush beef all over with mixture.
3 Place beef in medium oiled baking dish with beetroots; roast, uncovered, 10 minutes.
4 Reduce heat to 200°C/400°F; roast a further 20 minutes or until beef and beetroots are cooked. Cover beef; stand 15 minutes then slice thinly. Peel and halve beetroots.
5 Make parmesan croûtons. Make horseradish crème fraîche.
6 Combine beetroot, rocket, cucumber and parsley in large bowl. Serve salad topped with croûtons and beef; drizzle with horseradish crème fraîche.

PARMESAN CROÛTONS Slice bread thinly; brush slices with oil, place on oven tray. Brown, in oven, towards end of beef cooking time; sprinkle with cheese, return to oven until cheese melts.

HORSERADISH CRÈME FRAÎCHE Combine ingredients in small bowl.

prep + cook time 45 minutes (+ standing) serves 4
nutritional count per serving 33.8g total fat (12.2g saturated fat); 2704kJ (647 cal); 40.7g carbohydrate; 40.2g protein; 10.5g fibre

Crème fraîche, a fermented cream having a slightly tangy, nutty flavour and velvety texture, can be used in both sweet and savoury dishes, in much the same way as sour cream.

pork and caramelised apple salad

600g (1¼ pounds) pork fillets
2 tablespoons light brown sugar
2 teaspoons wholegrain mustard
2 teaspoons finely grated orange rind
1 tablespoon olive oil
10g (½ ounce) butter
1 medium green-skinned apple (150g), unpeeled,
   halved, cut into 5mm (¼ inch) thick slices
60g (2 ounces) baby spinach leaves

SPICED ORANGE DRESSING
¼ cup (60ml) olive oil
2 tablespoons orange juice
1 tablespoon cider vinegar
1 teaspoon ground mixed spice

1 Combine pork, sugar, mustard and rind in medium bowl.
2 Heat oil in medium frying pan; cook pork until cooked as desired. Cover pork; stand 5 minutes then slice thinly.
3 Melt butter in same frying pan; cook apple until caramelised.
4 Meanwhile, make spiced orange dressing.
5 Combine apple mixture, dressing and spinach in medium bowl. Arrange pork among serving plates; top with apple salad. Drizzle with any remaining dressing from bowl.

SPICED ORANGE DRESSING Combine ingredients in screw-top jar; shake well.

prep + cook time 35 minutes serves 4
nutritional count per serving 23.8g total fat
(5.1g saturated fat); 1639kJ (392 cal);
10.6g carbohydrate; 33.5g protein; 1.1g fibre

warm lamb and pasta provençale salad

375g (12 ounces) rigatoni pasta
600g (1¼ pounds) lamb fillets
¾ cup (115g) seeded black olives, halved
1 cup (150g) drained semi-dried tomatoes in oil,
   chopped coarsely
400g (12½ ounces) canned artichoke hearts,
   drained, halved
1 small red onion (100g), sliced thinly
60g (2 ounces) baby rocket leaves (arugula)
½ cup (120g) green olive tapenade
2 tablespoons olive oil
2 tablespoons lemon juice

1 Cook pasta in large saucepan of boiling water
until tender; drain.
2 Meanwhile, cook lamb, uncovered, in heated
oiled large frying pan until cooked as desired.
Cover lamb; stand 5 minutes then slice thickly.
3 Combine pasta with lamb and remaining
ingredients in large bowl.

prep + cook time 30 minutes **serves** 6
nutritional count per serving 16.9g total fat
(3.4g saturated fat); 2203kJ (527 cal);
57.4g carbohydrate; 32g protein; 7.5g fibre

Tortiglioni is a tubular pasta that's often served with thick sauces or in casseroles. You could use rigatoni or penne pasta instead of the tortiglioni. Any leftover bolognese sauce can be used to make this pasta salad.

warm creamy bolognese pasta salad

1 tablespoon olive oil
1 medium brown onion (150g), chopped finely
1 medium carrot (120g), chopped finely
1 celery stalk (150g), trimmed, chopped finely
500g (1 pound) minced (ground) beef
1 cup (250ml) milk
30g (1 ounce) butter
1 cup (250ml) beef stock
1 cup (260g) bottled tomato pasta sauce
½ cup (125ml) dry red wine
2 tablespoons tomato paste
2 tablespoons coarsely chopped fresh
   flat-leaf parsley
375g (12 ounces) tortiglioni pasta
½ cup (75g) drained semi-dried tomatoes in oil,
   chopped coarsely
90g (3 ounces) baby spinach leaves
4 green onions (scallions), sliced thinly

1 Heat oil in large saucepan; cook brown onion, carrot and celery, stirring, until carrot softens. Add beef; cook, stirring, until beef changes colour. Stir in milk and butter; cook, stirring occasionally, until liquid reduces by half. Add stock, pasta sauce, wine and paste; simmer, uncovered, about 1 hour or until sauce thickens. Remove from heat; stir in parsley. Cool 20 minutes.
2 Meanwhile, cook pasta in large saucepan of boiling water until tender; drain. Rinse under cold water; drain.
3 Combine pasta in large bowl with chopped tomato, spinach, green onion and beef mixture.

prep + cook time 1 hour 15 minutes (+ cooling)
serves 6
nutritional count per serving 5.6g total fat
(2.4g saturated fat); 610kJ (146 cal);
15.2g carbohydrate; 7.9g protein; 1.8g fibre

barbecued lamb, shallot and mesclun salad

150g (4½ ounces) sugar snap peas, trimmed
600g (1¼ pounds) lamb backstrap
8 large shallots (200g), peeled, quartered
60g (2 ounces) mesclun

MINT DRESSING
1 cup firmly packed fresh mint leaves
2 cloves garlic, quartered
¼ cup (60ml) olive oil
2 tablespoons white wine vinegar
2 teaspoons caster (superfine) sugar

1 Boil, steam or microwave peas until tender; drain.
2 Meanwhile, cook lamb and shallot on heated oiled grill plate (or grill or barbecue) until lamb is cooked as desired and shallot is tender. Cover lamb; stand 5 minutes then slice thinly.
3 Meanwhile, make mint dressing.
4 Combine peas, lamb, shallot, dressing and mesclun in large bowl.

MINT DRESSING Blend or process mint and garlic until smooth. With motor operating, gradually add oil in a thin, steady stream; blend until smooth. Stir in vinegar and sugar.

prep + cook time 25 minutes serves 4
nutritional count per serving 19.4g total fat (4.4g saturated fat); 1404kJ (336 cal); 6.2g carbohydrate; 33.2g protein; 2.7g fibre

If you can't find lamb backstrap, use lamb fillets instead.

lamb and fetta salad with warm walnut dressing

1 tablespoon vegetable oil
600g (1¼ pounds) lamb fillets
200g (6½ ounces) fetta cheese, crumbled
250g (8 ounces) witlof (belgian endive),
  leaves separated
150g (4½ ounces) baby spinach leaves

WARM WALNUT DRESSING
2 cloves garlic, crushed
1 teaspoon finely grated lemon rind
¼ cup (60ml) olive oil
2 tablespoons cider vinegar
½ cup (55g) coarsely chopped roasted walnuts

1   Heat oil in large frying pan; cook lamb until
cooked as desired. Cover lamb; stand 5 minutes
then slice thickly.
2   Make warm walnut dressing.
3   Combine lamb in medium bowl with cheese,
witlof and spinach; drizzle with dressing to serve.

WARM WALNUT DRESSING Cook garlic, rind, oil
and vinegar in small pan, stirring, until hot. Remove
from heat; stir in nuts.

prep + cook time 25 minutes serves 4
nutritional count per serving 52.8g total fat
(16.8g saturated fat); 2742kJ (656 cal);
1.2g carbohydrate; 43.8g protein; 3.2g fibre

pasta, pulse & grain salads

italian brown rice salad

3 cups (750ml) vegetable stock
2 teaspoons olive oil
1 small brown onion (80g), chopped finely
1½ cups (300g) brown medium-grain rice
1 teaspoon finely grated lime rind
1 clove garlic, crushed
⅓ cup (45g) roasted slivered almonds
⅔ cup (100g) sun-dried tomatoes, chopped coarsely
½ cup (60g) seeded black olives, chopped coarsely
½ cup coarsely chopped fresh basil
¼ cup coarsely chopped fresh flat-leaf parsley

LIME AND MUSTARD DRESSING
2 tablespoons lime juice
2 tablespoons white wine vinegar
2 cloves garlic, crushed
2 teaspoons dijon mustard

1 Place stock in medium saucepan; bring to the boil. Reduce heat; simmer, covered.
2 Meanwhile, heat oil in large saucepan; cook onion, stirring, until soft. Add rice, rind and garlic; stir to coat rice in onion mixture.
3 Add stock; bring to the boil. Reduce heat; simmer, covered, about 50 minutes or until rice is tender and liquid is absorbed.
4 Make lime and mustard dressing.
5 Add nuts, tomato, olives, basil and dressing to rice mixture in pan; toss gently to combine.
6 Serve salad warm; top with parsley.

LIME AND MUSTARD DRESSING Combine ingredients in screw-top jar; shake well.

prep + cook time 1 hour 15 minutes serves 4
nutritional count per serving 13.3g total fat
(1.8g saturated fat); 1923kJ (460 cal);
76.3g carbohydrate; 14.7g protein; 9.4g fibre

We used the sun-dried tomatoes that have not been preserved in oil; they are generally sold in plastic bags or loose by weight.

pumpkin ravioli and roasted tomato salad

500g (1 pound) cherry tomatoes, halved
2 medium red onions (340g), halved, sliced thinly
1 teaspoon caster (superfine) sugar
¼ cup (60ml) olive oil
1kg (2 pounds) pumpkin ravioli
100g (3 ounces) baby rocket leaves (arugula)
150g (4½ ounces) small black olives, seeded
2 tablespoons rinsed, drained baby capers
2 tablespoons red wine vinegar

1 Preheat oven to 220°C/425°F. Line oven tray with baking paper.
2 Place tomato and onion on tray in a single layer; sprinkle with sugar, drizzle with 1 tablespoon of the oil. Roast, uncovered, about 20 minutes.
3 Meanwhile, cook ravioli in large saucepan of boiling water until tender; drain.
4 Combine ravioli in large bowl with tomato, onion, rocket, olives and capers. Drizzle salad with combined vinegar and remaining oil.

prep + cook time 30 minutes **serves** 6
nutritional count per serving 18g total fat
(4.7g saturated fat); 1542kJ (369 cal);
35g carbohydrate; 14.3g protein; 5.2g fibre

Roasting the tomatoes concentrates the flavour, which goes well with pumpkin. Serve the salad warm.

warm crunchy rice salad

1 cup (200g) wild rice blend
1 medium red capsicum (bell pepper) (200g),
  sliced thinly
1 small red onion (100g), sliced thinly
⅓ cup (50g) sunflower seed kernels
⅓ cup (65g) pepitas (dried pumpkin seeds)
⅓ cup (50g) roasted unsalted cashews
½ cup coarsely chopped fresh flat-leaf parsley
2 tablespoons coarsely chopped fresh oregano

BLACK PEPPER DRESSING
1 teaspoon finely grated lemon rind
¼ cup (60ml) lemon juice
2 tablespoons olive oil
1 teaspoon dijon mustard
1 teaspoon cracked black pepper

1 Cook rice in large saucepan of boiling water,
uncovered, until just tender; drain. Rinse under
warm water; drain.
2 Meanwhile, make black pepper dressing.
3 Combine rice and dressing in large bowl with
remaining ingredients.

BLACK PEPPER DRESSING Combine ingredients
in screw-top jar; shake well.

prep + cook time 25 minutes **serves** 4
nutritional count per serving 27.4g total fat
(2.9g saturated fat); 1639kJ (392 cal);
15.7g carbohydrate; 8.3g protein; 6g fibre

Wild rice blend is a packaged mixture of white long-grain and dark
brown wild rice. The latter is the seed of a North American aquatic
grass, which has a distinctively nutty flavour and a crunchy, resilient
texture. It is available from most supermarkets.

Wild rice blend is a pre-made mixture of white long-grain and wild rices. It is available from most supermarkets.

greek-style wild rice salad

2 cups (400g) wild rice blend
1 medium red capsicum (bell pepper) (200g)
1 medium brown onion (150g), quartered
250g (8 ounces) cherry tomatoes
350g (11 ounces) broccolini, halved crossways
½ cup (80g) roasted pine nuts
1 cup coarsely chopped fresh flat-leaf parsley
2 tablespoons lemon juice

LEMON AND GARLIC YOGURT DRESSING
2 cloves garlic, crushed
300g (9½ ounces) yogurt
¼ cup (60ml) lemon juice

1 Make lemon and garlic yogurt dressing.
2 Cook rice in large saucepan of boiling water, uncovered, until tender; drain. Place in large serving bowl.
3 Quarter capsicum; discard seeds and membranes. Cook capsicum, onion and tomatoes on heated, oiled grill plate (or grill or barbecue) until tender. Chop capsicum and onion coarsely.
4 Boil, steam or microwave broccolini until tender.
5 Combine capsicum, onion, tomatoes, nuts, parsley and juice with rice. Serve salad topped with broccolini then dressing.

LEMON AND GARLIC YOGURT DRESSING
Combine ingredients in small bowl.

prep + cook time 25 minutes **serves** 6
nutritional count per serving 11.6g total fat (1.7g saturated fat); 1007kJ (241 cal); 20.2g carbohydrate; 10.9g protein; 6.3g fibre

couscous, carrot and pistachio pilaf

2 cups (500ml) water
2 cups (400g) couscous
1 small red onion (100g), chopped finely
1 tablespoon olive oil
2 large carrots (360g), sliced thinly
1 cup (120g) pimiento-stuffed green olives, halved
½ cup (70g) roasted unsalted pistachios,
  chopped coarsely
420g (13½ ounces) canned chickpeas (garbanzos),
  rinsed, drained
1 cup loosely packed fresh coriander leaves
  (cilantro)

SUMAC DRESSING
⅓ cup (80ml) olive oil
½ cup (125ml) lemon juice
3 teaspoons sumac

1   Bring the water to the boil in medium saucepan.
Remove from heat; stir in couscous and onion.
Cover; stand about 5 minutes or until liquid is
absorbed, fluffing with fork occasionally.
2   Meanwhile, heat oil in large frying pan; cook
carrot, covered, about 3 minutes or until just
tender. Uncover; cook a further 3 minutes.
3   Make sumac dressing.
4   Combine couscous mixture with carrot, dressing
and remaining ingredients in large bowl.

SUMAC DRESSING   Combine ingredients in
screw-top jar; shake well.

prep + cook time 25 minutes serves 4
nutritional count per serving 36.3g total fat
(4.9g saturated fat); 3436kJ (822 cal);
95.9g carbohydrate; 22.4g protein; 11g fibre

If you can't find orecchiette, replace it with penne, the quill-shaped pasta.

warm pasta, pea and ricotta salad

375g (12 ounces) orecchiette pasta
1½ cups (200g) frozen baby peas
½ cup coarsely chopped fresh mint
100g (3 ounces) shaved ham, chopped coarsely
1 teaspoon finely grated lemon rind
200g (6½ ounces) ricotta cheese, crumbled

BUTTERMILK AÏOLI
⅓ cup (100g) mayonnaise
2 tablespoons buttermilk
2 teaspoons lemon juice
1 clove garlic, crushed
1 teaspoon finely grated lemon rind

1   Cook pasta in large saucepan of boiling water until tender. Add peas during last 2 minutes of pasta cooking time; drain.
2   Meanwhile, make buttermilk aïoli.
3   Combine warm pasta, peas, mint, ham, rind and aïoli in large bowl. Serve salad sprinkled with cheese.

BUTTERMILK AÏOLI Combine ingredients in small bowl.

prep + cook time 25 minutes serves 4
nutritional count per serving 16.2g total fat (5.2g saturated fat); 2328kJ (557 cal); 74.5g carbohydrate; 24.3g protein; 6.8g fibre

moroccan couscous salad

1½ cups (300g) couscous
1½ cups (375ml) boiling water
20g (¾ ounce) butter
420g (13½ ounces) canned chickpeas (garbanzos),
  rinsed, drained
⅓ cup (55g) sultanas
⅓ cup (50g) roasted pine nuts
100g (3 ounces) baby rocket leaves (arugula),
  chopped coarsely
¾ cup finely chopped fresh flat-leaf parsley
1 cup (120g) seeded green olives

PRESERVED LEMON DRESSING
1 tablespoon finely grated lemon rind
¼ cup (60ml) lemon juice
¼ cup (60ml) olive oil
2 tablespoons finely chopped preserved lemon rind

1 Combine couscous with the water in large heatproof bowl, cover; stand about 5 minutes or until liquid is absorbed, fluffing with fork occasionally. Stir in butter; stand 10 minutes.
2 Make preserved lemon dressing.
3 Combine couscous in large bowl with remaining ingredients and dressing.

PRESERVED LEMON DRESSING Combine ingredients in screw-top jar; shake well.

prep time 20 minutes serves 4
nutritional count per serving 29g total fat (5.5g saturated fat); 268kJ (686 cal); 85.6g carbohydrate; 17.2g protein; 6.5g fibre

note Preserved lemon is a North African speciality, where lemons, whole or sliced, are placed in a mixture of salt and oil or lemon juice. To use, remove and discard pulp, squeeze juice from rind; rinse rind well, then slice it thinly.

pasta salad with fried sprouts, bocconcini and almonds

500g (1 pound) rigatoni pasta
1 tablespoon olive oil
300g (9½ ounces) brussels sprouts, trimmed, shredded coarsely
½ cup coarsely chopped fresh flat-leaf parsley
1 tablespoon rinsed, drained capers
200g (6½ ounces) bocconcini cheese, sliced thickly
½ cup (80g) roasted almonds, chopped coarsely

RED WINE VINAIGRETTE
⅓ cup (80ml) lemon juice
⅓ cup (80ml) red wine vinegar
¼ cup (60ml) olive oil
1 teaspoon white sugar
2 cloves garlic, crushed

1   Make red wine vinaigrette.
2   Cook pasta in large saucepan of boiling water until just tender; drain. Place in large serving bowl.
3   Heat oil in same pan; stir-fry sprouts about 1 minute or until just warm.
4   Combine sprouts and remaining ingredients with pasta and vinaigrette; mix gently.

RED WINE VINAIGRETTE Combine ingredients in screw-top jar; shake well.

prep + cook time 25 minutes serves 6
nutritional count per serving 25.7g total fat
(5.7g saturated fat); 2358kJ (564 cal);
60g carbohydrate; 19.9g protein; 6.2g fibre

roasted egg tomatoes with barley salad

1 cup (200g) pearl barley
4 medium egg (plum) tomatoes (300g), cut into thick wedges
2 small green capsicum (bell pepper) (300g), chopped finely
1 small red onion (100g), chopped finely
⅔ cup coarsely chopped fresh flat-leaf parsley

LEMON AND DILL DRESSING
¼ cup (60ml) lemon juice
1½ tablespoons finely chopped fresh dill
1 tablespoon olive oil
1 clove garlic, crushed

1 Preheat oven to 240°C/475°F.
2 Cook barley in small saucepan of boiling water, uncovered, about 20 minutes or until just tender; drain. Rinse under cold water; drain.
3 Meanwhile, place tomato, cut-side up, on lightly oiled oven tray. Roast tomato, uncovered, about 15 minutes or until just softened.
4 Make lemon and dill dressing.
5 Place barley and half the tomato in medium bowl with capsicum, onion, parsley and dressing; toss gently to combine. Top with remaining tomato.

LEMON AND DILL DRESSING Combine ingredients in screw-top jar; shake well.

prep + cook time 45 minutes **serves** 4
nutritional count per serving 6g total fat (0.8g saturated fat); 1003kJ (240 cal); 35.3g carbohydrate; 6.6g protein; 8.1g fibre

Pearl barley is a nutritious grain that has had the husk removed, and then has been hulled and polished so only the 'pearl' of the original grain remains, much the same as white rice. It is available from health-food stores and most supermarkets.

borlotti bean, brown rice and almond salad

1 cup (200g) dried borlotti beans
1 cup (200g) brown long-grain rice
1 small red onion (100g), chopped finely
1 cup finely chopped fresh flat-leaf parsley
1 cup finely chopped fresh mint
3 medium tomatoes (450g), chopped finely
2 tablespoons roasted slivered almonds
¼ cup (60ml) lemon juice
1 tablespoon olive oil

1 Place beans in small bowl, cover with water; stand overnight, drain. Rinse under cold water; drain.
2 Cook beans in small saucepan of boiling water, uncovered, until just tender; drain. Rinse under cold water; drain.
3 Meanwhile, cook rice in small saucepan of boiling water, uncovered, until rice is tender; drain. Rinse under cold water; drain.
4 Place beans and rice in medium bowl with remaining ingredients; toss gently to combine.

prep + cook time 45 minutes (+ standing) **serves** 4
nutritional count per serving 10.6g total fat
(1.3g saturated fat); 1584kJ (379 cal);
61.3g carbohydrate; 18.7g protein; 16.3g fibre

chickpea and lentil salad

¾ cup sun-dried tomatoes in oil (105g), drained, chopped coarsely

¼ cup (60ml) olive oil

1 tablespoon lemon juice

415g (13 ounces) canned brown lentils, rinsed, drained

410g (13 ounces) canned chickpeas (garbanzos), rinsed, drained

250g (8 ounces) silver beet (swiss chard), trimmed, shredded finely

1 To make dressing, blend or process ¼ cup of the tomatoes, oil and juice until finely chopped.

2 Combine lentils, chickpeas, silver beet, half the sun-dried tomato dressing and remaining sun-dried tomatoes in large bowl; season to taste.

3 Top with remaining dressing.

prep time 15 minutes **serves** 4
nutritional count per serving 16.7g total fat (2.3g saturated fat); 1325kJ (317 cal); 24.8g carbohydrate; 11.8g protein; 10.7g fibre

note Spinach can be used in place of silver beet.

warm lentil and chorizo salad

1¼ cups (250g) french-style green lentils
1 small brown onion (80g), quartered
1 dried bay leaf
2 cured chorizo sausages (340g), sliced thinly
3 shallots (75g), sliced thinly
2 celery stalks (300g), trimmed, sliced diagonally
1 cup coarsely chopped fresh flat-leaf parsley

MACADAMIA DRESSING
½ cup (125ml) red wine vinegar
⅓ cup (80ml) macadamia oil

1 Cook lentils, onion and bay leaf in large saucepan of boiling water, uncovered, about 15 minutes or until lentils are tender; drain. Discard onion and bay leaf.
2 Cook chorizo in large frying pan, stirring occasionally, until browned. Drain; cool 10 minutes.
3 Make macadamia dressing.
4 Combine lentils and chorizo in large bowl with shallot, celery, parsley and dressing.

MACADAMIA DRESSING Combine ingredients in screw-top jar; shake well.

prep + cook time 40 minutes serves 4
nutritional count per serving 30.2g total fat (8.1g saturated fat); 1860kJ (445 cal); 19.1g carbohydrate; 21.8g protein; 7.3g fibre

note French-style green lentils are related to the famous french lentils du puy; these green-blue, tiny lentils have a nutty, earthy flavour and a hardy nature that allows them to be rapidly cooked without disintegrating. They are also known as australian, bondi or matilda lentils.

mixed bean salad

2 cloves garlic, crushed
1 tablespoon olive oil
2 tablespoons lemon juice
420g (13½ ounces) canned four-bean mix,
  rinsed, drained
2 celery stalks (300g), trimmed, chopped finely
2 small yellow capsicum (bell pepper) (300g),
  chopped finely
¾ cup (90g) seeded black olives, chopped coarsely
⅔ cup loosely packed fresh flat-leaf parsley leaves
1 small red onion (100g), sliced thinly
45g (1½ ounces) baby rocket leaves (arugula)

1 Combine garlic, oil and juice in screw-top jar;
shake well.
2 Place remaining ingredients and dressing
in medium bowl; toss gently to combine.

prep time 35 minutes **serves** 4
nutritional count per serving 5.4g total fat
(0.8g saturated fat); 694kJ (166 cal);
19.7g carbohydrate; 6.5g protein; 6.9g fibre

thai soya bean salad with grapes and pink grapefruit

1 cup (200g) dried soya beans
2 small ruby red grapefruit (700g), segmented
150g (4½ ounces) green grapes, halved
1 small white onion (80g), chopped finely
150g (4½ ounces) snow pea sprouts, trimmed
⅔ cup finely chopped fresh coriander (cilantro)
⅔ cup finely chopped fresh mint
2 fresh kaffir lime leaves, shredded finely
¼ cup (60ml) lime juice

1 Place beans in small bowl, cover with water; stand overnight, drain. Rinse under cold water; drain.
2 Cook beans in small saucepan of boiling water, uncovered, until just tender; drain. Rinse under cold water; drain.
3 Place beans in medium bowl with remaining ingredients; toss gently to combine.

prep + cook time 45 minutes (+ standing) **serves** 4
nutritional count per serving 10.6g total fat
(1.5g saturated fat); 1137kJ (272cal);
20.7g carbohydrate; 18.7g protein; 13g fibre

Ruby red grapefruit may sometimes be sold as pink grapefruit.

glossary

ARTICHOKE HEARTS tender centre of the globe artichoke; purchased in brine canned or in glass jars.

ASIAN GREENS, MIXED BABY mix of baby buk choy, choy sum, gai lan and water spinach. Available from Asian food stores and selected supermarkets.

BACON from cured, smoked pork side.

BAKING PAPER also parchment paper or baking parchment – a silicone-coated paper primarily used for lining baking pans and oven trays so cakes and biscuits won't stick.

BEANS

borlotti also known as roman beans or pink beans, available fresh or dried. Interchangeable with pinto beans because of the similarity in appearance – both are pale pink or beige with dark red streaks.

butter also known as lima beans; large, flat, kidney-shaped bean, off-white in colour, with a mealy texture and mild taste. Available canned and dried.

four-bean mix a mix of kidney, butter and cannellini beans, and chickpeas.

soya low in carbohydrates and high in protein; the source of products such as tofu, soy milk, soy sauce, tamari and miso. Available dried and canned; sometimes sold fresh as edamame.

BEETROOT known as red beets or just beets; firm, round root vegetable.

BREAD

ciabatta in Italian, the word means 'slipper', which is the traditional shape of this crisp crusted white bread.

french stick bread that's been formed into a long, narrow, cylindrical loaf. Usually has a crisp brown crust and a light chewy interior. Also known as french bread, french loaf or baguette.

pitta also known as lebanese bread. A wheat-flour pocket bread sold in large, flat pieces that separate into two thin rounds. Also available in small thick pieces called pocket pitta.

sourdough has a lightly sour taste from the yeast starter culture used to make the bread. A low-risen bread with a dense centre and crisp crust.

BREADCRUMBS, PACKAGED fine-textured, crunchy, purchased white breadcrumbs.

BURGHUL made from whole wheat kernels that are steamed, dried and toasted before cracking into several distinct sizes, so they develop a rich, nutty flavour. Because it is already partially cooked, burghul only requires minimal cooking. Cracked wheat, on the other hand, is raw whole wheat.

BUTTERMILK originally the term given to the slightly sour liquid left after butter was churned from cream, today it is commercially made similarly to yogurt. Sold in the refrigerated dairy compartment in supermarkets. Despite the implication of its name, it is low in fat.

CAPSICUM also known as bell pepper or, simply, pepper; comes in green, red, yellow, orange and purplish-black colours. Discard membranes and seeds before using.

CHAR-GRILLED ANTIPASTO marinated char-grilled vegetables that usually include capsicum, eggplant and zucchini and other vegetables.

CHEESE

blue mould-treated cheeses mottled with blue veining. Varieties include firm and crumbly stilton types to mild, creamy brie-like cheeses.

bocconcini from the diminutive of boccone meaning 'mouthful'; is the term used for walnut-sized, baby mozzarella. A delicate, semi-soft, white cheese traditionally made in Italy from buffalo milk. Spoils rapidly so must be kept under refrigeration, in brine, for 1 or 2 days at most. *Cherry bocconcini* are even smaller in size.

fetta Greek in origin; a crumbly textured goat- or sheep-milk cheese with a sharp, salty taste.

haloumi a firm, cream-coloured sheep-milk cheese matured in brine. Somewhat like a minty, salty fetta in flavour, haloumi can be grilled or fried, briefly, without breaking down. It should be eaten while still warm as it becomes tough and rubbery on cooling.

parmesan also known as parmigiana; a hard, grainy, cows'-milk cheese that originated in the Parma region of Italy. The curd is salted in brine for a month before being aged for up to two years in humid conditions.

ricotta soft, white, cows'-milk cheese; roughly translates as 'cooked again'. It's made from whey, a by-product of other cheese making, to which fresh milk and acid are added. Ricotta is a sweet, moist cheese with a slightly grainy texture.

CHICKPEAS also called garbanzos, hummus or channa; an irregularly round, sandy-coloured legume.

CHILLI available in many different types and sizes. Use rubber gloves when seeding and chopping fresh chillies as they can burn your skin. Removing seeds and membranes lessens the heat level.

flakes dried, deep-red, dehydrated chilli slices and whole seeds.

long red available both fresh and dried; a generic term used for any moderately hot, long, thin chilli (about 6-8cm/2½-3 inches long).

red thai also known as 'scuds'; tiny, hot and bright red in colour.

CHINESE BARBECUED DUCK traditionally cooked in special ovens, this duck has a sweet-sticky coating made from soy sauce, five-spice, sherry and hoisin sauce. It is available from Asian food stores.

CHINESE BARBECUED PORK also called char siew. Traditionally cooked in special ovens, this pork has a sweet-sticky coating made from soy and hoisin sauces, sherry and five-spice powder. Available from Asian food stores.

CHINESE COOKING WINE also known as shao hsing or chinese rice wine. Inexpensive and found in Asian food shops; if you can't find it, replace with mirin or sherry.

CHORIZO SAUSAGES Spanish in origin; made of coarsely ground pork and highly seasoned with garlic and chilli. They are deeply smoked, very spicy and dry-cured. Also available raw.

COUSCOUS a fine, grain-like cereal product made from semolina. A dough of semolina flour and water is sieved then dehydrated to produce minuscule even-sized pellets of couscous; it is rehydrated by steaming, or with the addition of a warm liquid, and swells to three or four times its original size.

CREAM, POURING we used fresh cream, also known as pure or single cream, unless otherwise stated.

CRÈME FRAÎCHE mature fermented cream with a slightly tangy, nutty flavour and velvety texture. Can boil without curdling and can be used in both sweet and savoury dishes.

DILL PICKLE a small cucumber that's been preserved in brine or vinegar flavoured with dill seeds.

EGGPLANT, BABY also known as finger or japanese eggplant; very small and slender so can be used without disgorging (salting to remove any bitter juices).

EGGS some recipes in this book call for raw or barely cooked eggs; exercise caution if there's a salmonella problem in your area, particularly in food eaten by children and pregnant women.

FLOUR
plain an all-purpose wheat flour.
rice a very fine flour made from ground white rice.

FRIED SHALLOTS served at Asian mealtimes as a condiment or sprinkled over just-cooked food to provide an extra crunchy finish. Available at Asian grocery stores. Make your own by frying peeled, thinly sliced shallots or baby onions until golden brown and crisp.

GINGER also known as green or root ginger; the thick root of a tropical plant. *Pickled ginger* is sold in pieces or sliced, and comes in red and pink varieties packed in a mixture of vinegar, sugar and natural colouring.

GRAPEFRUIT the largest available citrus fruit, grapefruit are available with or without seeds; the seeded variety has more flavour. *Ruby* or *ruby red grapefruit* (also known as *pink grapefruit*) is a pink-fleshed version.

GREEN MANGO sour and crunchy, green mangoes are just immature fruit. They will keep, wrapped in plastic, in the fridge for up to two weeks. They are available at Asian food stores;

GREEN PAPAYA are just unripe papayas. They are available at Asian food stores; look for one that is hard and slightly shiny, proving it is freshly picked. Papaya will ripen rapidly if not used within a day or two.

HORSERADISH
cream a creamy paste made of grated horseradish, vinegar, oil and sugar.
preserved grated horseradish root.

KAFFIR LIME LEAVES also known as bai magrood; sold fresh, dried or frozen. Dried leaves are less potent, so double the number called for in a recipe if you substitute them for fresh leaves. A strip of fresh lime peel may be substituted for each kaffir lime leaf.

KECAP MANIS *see sauces, soy.*

KUMARA name of an orange-fleshed sweet potato often confused with yam.

LEMON GRASS a tall, clumping, lemon-smelling and -tasting, sharp-edged grass; the white lower part of each stem is chopped and used in Asian cooking.

LENTILS (red, brown, yellow) dried pulses often identified by, and named after, their colour.
french-style green lentils related to the famous french lentils du puy; these green-blue, tiny lentils have a nutty, earthy flavour and a hardy nature that allows them to be rapidly cooked without disintegrating. Also known as australian, bondi or matilda lentils.

LETTUCE *see 'Salad Greens' page 6.*

LYCHEES small fruit from China with a hard shell and sweet, juicy flesh. The white flesh has a gelatinous texture and musky, perfumed taste. Discard the rough skin and seed before using.

MAPLE SYRUP a thin syrup distilled from the sap of the maple tree. Maple-flavoured syrup or pancake syrup is not an adequate substitute for the real thing.

MUSHROOMS
button small, cultivated white mushrooms with a mild flavour.
flat large, flat mushrooms with a rich earthy flavour, ideal for filling and barbecuing. They are sometimes misnamed field mushrooms, which are wild mushrooms.

NASHI more commonly known as the Asian pear. A member of the pear family but resembling an apple with its pale yellow-green, tennis-ball sized appearance.

PANCETTA an Italian-style bacon; cured but not smoked.

PAPPADUMS sun-dried wafers made from a combination of lentil and rice flours, oil and spices.

PASTA
farfalle bow-tie shaped short pasta; sometimes known as butterfly pasta.
orecchiette small disc-shaped pasta; translates literally as 'little ears'.
rigatoni a tube-shaped, flat-ended, ridged pasta. Is larger than penne.

PEPITAS edible pumpkin seeds that have had their white hull removed; are green, with a delicate nutty flavour.

PIMIENTO-STUFFED GREEN OLIVES a green olive with a lively, briny bitterness containing a morsel of capsicum, which adds a flash of colour.

PINE NUTS also known as pignoli; not, in fact, a nut, but a small, cream-coloured kernel from pine cones.

POMEGRANATE dark-red, leathery-skinned fruit about the size of an orange filled with hundreds of seeds, each wrapped in an edible lucent-crimson pulp having a tangy sweet-sour flavour.

POMEGRANATE MOLASSES has tart and fruity qualities similar to balsamic vinegar. Is thicker, browner and more concentrated in flavour than grenadine, the sweet, red pomegranate syrup used in cocktails. Available at Middle Eastern food stores, specialty food shops and better delicatessens.

POTATOES, BABY NEW also known as chats; an early harvest with thin skin.

PROSCIUTTO a kind of unsmoked Italian ham; salted, air-cured and aged, it is usually eaten uncooked.

QUAIL small, delicately flavoured, domestically-grown game birds ranging in weight from 250-300g (8-10 ounces); also known as partridge.

SAMBAL OELEK (also ulek or olek) Indonesian in origin; a salty paste made from ground chillies and vinegar.

SAUCES
cranberry, whole berry made of cranberries cooked in sugar syrup; has an astringent flavour.
fish also called nam pla or nuoc nam; made from pulverised salted fermented fish, most often anchovies. Has a strong taste and pungent smell; use sparingly.
oyster Asian in origin, this rich, brown sauce is made from oysters and their brine, cooked with salt and soy sauce, and thickened with starches.
plum a thick sauce made from plums, vinegar, sugar, chillies and spices.
soy made from fermented soya beans. Several variations are available in most supermarkets and Asian food stores.
dark soy deep brown, almost black in colour; rich, with a thicker consistency than other types. Pungent but not very salty; it is good for marinating.
japanese soy all-purpose low-sodium soy sauce made with more wheat content than its Chinese counterparts; fermented in barrels and aged. Possibly the best table soy and the one to choose if you only want one variety.
kecap manis a dark, thick, sweet soy sauce. The sweetness is derived from the addition of either molasses or palm sugar when brewed.
light soy fairly thin and, while paler than the others, is the saltiest tasting; used in dishes where the natural colour of the ingredients is to be maintained. Not to be confused with salt-reduced or low-sodium soy sauces.
tamari a thick, dark soy sauce made mainly from soya beans without the wheat used in standard soy sauce.
tomato also known as ketchup or catsup; made from tomatoes, vinegar and spices.

tomato pasta made from a blend of tomatoes, herbs and spices.
worcestershire a dark coloured sauce made from tamarind, molasses, lime, onions, garlic, soy, anchovies, vinegar and seasonings.

SHALLOTS also called french shallots, golden shallots or eschalots; small, elongated, brown-skinned members of the onion family. Grows in tight clusters similar to garlic.

SPICES
cinnamon stick dried inner bark of the shoots of the cinnamon tree.
coriander seeds have a mild, lemon-like taste that compliments both sweet and savoury dishes. *Ground coriander* is found in sweet mixed spice blends for cakes and biscuits as well as being used to thicken and flavour curries.
cumin a spice also known as zeera or comino; has a spicy, nutty flavour.
five-spice powder a fragrant mixture of ground cinnamon, cloves, star anise, sichuan pepper and fennel seeds. Also known as chinese five-spice.
ginger ground or powdered ginger is used as a flavouring in cakes and pies etc; can't be substituted for fresh ginger.
mixed spice a blend of ground spices usually consisting of cinnamon, allspice and nutmeg.
star anise the dried star-shaped fruit of a tree native to China. The pods have an astringent aniseed or licorice flavour. Is an essential ingredient in five-spice powder.
sumac a purple-red spice ground from the berries of a small Mediterranean shrub. Adds a tart, lemony flavour.

SUGAR
brown very soft, finely granulated sugar retaining molasses for colour and flavour.
caster also known as superfine or finely granulated table sugar.
palm also known as jaggery or gula melaka; made from the sap of the sugar palm tree. Light brown to dark-brown in colour and usually sold in rock-hard cakes; substitute it with brown sugar if unavailable.
white a coarse, granulated table sugar; also known as crystal sugar.

SULTANAS dried grapes; also known as golden raisins.

TAMARI *see sauces, soy.*

TAMARIND CONCENTRATE is the product of a tropical African tree. Thick and purple-black, it is ready-to-use; gives a sweet-sour, astringent taste to food. Found in Asian food stores.

TAPENADE a classic olive paste from the Provençe region of southern France; made from a blend of capers, olives, anchovies and olive oil.

TOMATOES
cherry also known as tiny tim or tom thumb tomatoes; small and round.
grape about the size of a grape; they can be oblong, pear or grape-shaped.
paste triple-concentrated tomato puree.
teardrop small pear-shaped tomatoes.
semi-dried partially dried tomato pieces in olive oil; softer and juicier than sun-dried. Are not a preserve, so do not keep as long as sun-dried.
sun-dried tomato pesto a thick paste made from sun-dried tomatoes, oil, vinegar and herbs.

VINEGAR
balsamic made from the juice of Trebbiano grapes; has a deep rich brown colour and a sweet/sour flavour.
balsamic white vinegar (condiment) a clear and lighter version of balsamic vinegar; has a fresh, sweet clean taste.
cider (apple cider) made from the pulp of fermented apples.
raspberry made from fresh raspberries steeped in a white wine vinegar.
red wine based on fermented red wine.
rice a colourless vinegar made from fermented rice and flavoured with sugar and salt. Also known as seasoned rice vinegar.
rice wine made from rice wine lees (sediment left after fermentation), salt and alcohol.
white made from spirit of cane sugar.
white wine made from a blend of white wines.

ZUCCHINI also known as courgette; small, pale- or dark-green, yellow or white vegetable belonging to the squash family. Its flowers are edible if harvested when young.

conversion chart

MEASURES

One Australian metric measuring cup holds approximately 250ml; one Australian metric tablespoon holds 20ml; one Australian metric teaspoon holds 5ml.

The difference between one country's measuring cups and another's is within a two- or three-teaspoon variance, and will not affect your cooking results. North America, New Zealand and the United Kingdom use a 15ml tablespoon.

All cup and spoon measurements are level. The most accurate way of measuring dry ingredients is to weigh them. When measuring liquids, use a clear glass or plastic jug with the metric markings.

We use large eggs with an average weight of 60g.

The imperial measurements used in these recipes are approximate only.

DRY MEASURES

METRIC	IMPERIAL
15g	½oz
30g	1oz
60g	2oz
90g	3oz
125g	4oz (¼lb)
155g	5oz
185g	6oz
220g	7oz
250g	8oz (½lb)
280g	9oz
315g	10oz
345g	11oz
375g	12oz (¾lb)
410g	13oz
440g	14oz
470g	15oz
500g	16oz (1lb)
750g	24oz (1½lb)
1kg	32oz (2lb)

LIQUID MEASURES

METRIC	IMPERIAL
30ml	1 fluid oz
60ml	2 fluid oz
100ml	3 fluid oz
125ml	4 fluid oz
150ml	5 fluid oz
190ml	6 fluid oz
250ml	8 fluid oz
300ml	10 fluid oz
500ml	16 fluid oz
600ml	20 fluid oz
1000ml (1 litre)	1¾ pints

LENGTH MEASURES

METRIC	IMPERIAL
3mm	⅛in
6mm	¼in
1cm	½in
2cm	¾in
2.5cm	1in
5cm	2in
6cm	2½in
8cm	3in
10cm	4in
13cm	5in
15cm	6in
18cm	7in
20cm	8in
23cm	9in
25cm	10in
28cm	11in
30cm	12in (1ft)

OVEN TEMPERATURES

The oven temperatures in this book are for conventional ovens; if you have a fan-forced oven, decrease the temperature by 10-20 degrees.

	°C (CELSIUS)	°F (FAHRENHEIT)
Very slow	120	250
Slow	150	300
Moderately slow	160	325
Moderate	180	350
Moderately hot	200	400
Hot	220	425
Very hot	240	475

index

First published in 2011 by ACP Magazines Ltd,
a division of Nine Entertainment Co.
54 Park St, Sydney
GPO Box 4088, Sydney, NSW 2001.
phone (02) 9282 8618; fax (02) 9267 9438
acpbooks@acpmagazines.com.au; www.acpbooks.com.au

ACP BOOKS
General Manager - Christine Whiston
Editor-in-Chief - Susan Tomnay
Creative Director - Hieu Chi Nguyen
Food Director - Pamela Clark

Published and Distributed in the United Kingdom by Octopus Publishing Group
Endeavour House
189 Shaftesbury Avenue
London WC2H 8JY
United Kingdom
phone (+44)(0)207 632 5400; fax (+44)(0) 207 632 5405
info@octopus-publishing.co.uk;
www.octopusbooks.co.uk

Printed by Toppan Printing Co., China

International foreign language rights, Brian Cearnes, ACP Books bcearnes@acpmagazines.com.au

A catalogue record for this book is available from the British Library.
ISBN 978-1-907428-38-8
© ACP Magazines Ltd 2011
ABN 18 053 273 546